learn
to BURN

TABLE COASTERS, PAGE 32

learn
to
BURN

A Step-by-Step Guide to Getting Started in Pyrography

Simon Easton

Fox Chapel
PUBLISHING

© 2013 by Simon Easton and Fox Chapel Publishing Company, Inc., East Petersburg, PA.

ISBN 978-1-56523-728-5

Library of Congress Cataloging-in-Publication Data

Easton, Simon.
  Learn to burn : a step-by-step guide to getting started in pyrography / Simon Easton.
     pages cm
  Includes index.
  ISBN 978-1-56523-728-5 (pbk.)
  1. Pyrography. I. Title.
  TT199.8.E275 2013
  745.51'4--dc23
                          2012026300

To learn more about the other great books from Fox Chapel Publishing, or to find a retailer near you, call toll-free 800-457-9112 or visit us at *www.FoxChapelPublishing.com*.

Note to Authors: We are always looking for talented authors to write new books. Please send a brief letter describing your idea to Acquisition Editor, 1970 Broad Street, East Petersburg, PA 17520.

Printed in China
First printing

Dedication

This book is dedicated, as always, with my appreciation to the following people:

With love, to my beautiful wife, Jane, for inspiring me to be the best that I can be.

To my gorgeous daughter, Bethan, and my stepsons, Howell, Harry, and Freddie. Bethan won't be happy unless I mention our Jack Russell, too... so thanks, Pickle!

To all my true friends out there—those who continue to walk in when the rest of the world walks out. You know who you are, but a special mention goes out to Chailey Illman, Tim Emery, Jason Murphy, Michelle Wolfenden, Barry Walker, Sarah Preston, Sam MacArthur, Rhys Miles, Alex Marshall, and Nigel Woodall.

From a crafty perspective, I'd like to thank Peg Couch, Kerri Landis, Katie Weeber, Mindy Kinsey, and the team at Fox Chapel Publishing; Chailey Illman for the additional patterns provided; Lindsey White at Splatt Art; Cam Merkle at Razertip; Christine Wallace at Walnut Hollow; Colin Ellis at Dalescraft; Jeff Govier at The Big Wood; Pete Moncrieff-Jury at Bodrighy Wood; Steve Jardine at Craftshapes; Heather Smith at Beadbubble; Colin and Ann Carlson at Woodworks Crafts Supplies Ltd.; my fellow moderators at the UK Crafts Forum...and in fond memory of the Beadsage himself, Peter Sewell.

And to all those with a preference for the handmade and handcrafted, particularly the members of the online forums and websites who've made contact or visited my pages—please enjoy!

About the Author

Simon Easton studied a BA (Hons) Three-Dimensional Design degree at Manchester Metropolitan University, where he focussed on woodturning, silversmithing, and pewterware. His pewter napkin ring set was one of the MMU winners of the Pewter Live 1999 competition, and was displayed at Pewterers' Hall in London. He won both a Precious Metals Bursary and a Grant from the Worshipful Company of Goldsmiths in order to produce design concepts he had developed. The common theme in Simon's work was a decorative and textural feel, often rich in embellishment or pattern.

Before graduating in 2000, Simon's design for a wooden turned decorative bowl was selected for inclusion in the *onetree* project. This project, which toured the UK as an exhibition, stemmed from the use of one single ailing oak tree distributed to a range of artists, designers, manufacturers, and craftspeople. Every single part of the tree (from the leaves to the roots) was used to create a stirring and diverse display of talent, which was also featured in a book published to accompany the tour. For the *onetree* exhibition, Simon created a decorative turned wooden bowl with a spun pewter insert, entitled *Wish, Hope, Dream, Everything.*

In recent years, Simon's crafting focus and love of wood has led him to the art of pyrography, which he uses with a contemporary twist to create richly decorative items and gifts. The result is a diverse and exciting body of work released under the name *Wood Tattoos.* He has created a varied range of works and commissions, sells at craft fairs and galleries, and accepts custom orders at *www.woodtattoos.com.* He is an active member and moderator of the UK Crafts Forum, where he assists in passing on tips and advice to all craftspeople.

Simon is the author of *Woodburning with Style*, a comprehensive guide to the art of pyrography, published in 2010. The book has received many positive reviews from readers around the world. You can also see Simon's latest work by following him on *www.facebook.com/woodtattoos* and checking out his latest designs at *www.flickr.com/photos/woodtattoos*, where new photos are added regularly.

Contents

Get Started with Pyrography

Practice creating various shapes and lines, page 20.

Learn to shade with solid tones, as well as textures and patterns, page 21.

Find a list of the most important nibs, page 16.

Understand the features of your pyrography machine, page 19.

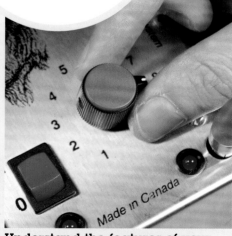

Learn the importance of the right pyrography pen, page 14.

Understand the benefits of mirroring text for easy design transfer, page 24.

Understand applying color, page 53.

Create designs with a three-dimensional feel, page 36.

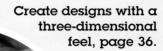

Enhance designs with texture and shading, page 58.

Learn how to wrap patterns around a box, page 50.

Understand how to create a shadow effect, page 30.

Learn to burn crisp letters, page 26.

Introduction

The publication of my first book, *Woodburning with Style*, was literally a dream come true. As an avid lover of books from an early age, I had always wanted to write a book—an ambition that ran alongside my creative streak and involvement in art, craft, and design. From childhood onward, I was always drawing, making, and constructing. I would always have a project of some sort on the go! I never anticipated that one day I would not only be able to realize my dream of becoming an author, but that my first book would also present one of my creative skills to the world in order to teach and instruct others wishing to learn the same skill.

Using pyrography to create the designs and items that I make is such a rewarding process, but the release of *Woodburning with Style* provided me with another source of satisfaction. After reading reviews on websites, Internet forums, and the like, I realized I was inspiring other budding craftspeople to think creatively and develop their newfound skills in order to turn their ideas into real works of art. I read the comments of people who had studied my book, recreated some of my ideas or projects to hone their pyrography skills, and were now excitedly planning their own individual designs due to the possibilities brimming in their heads.

That was truly the most exciting realization for me—my ideas, worked over for nearly two years prior to publication, were now reproduced and inspiring new ideas in others, forming new creative ventures that had needed a small nudge before they could be born in the real world. This suddenly made the whole project of my first book even more worthwhile in my mind, and it also spawned the reasoning behind the book that you now hold in your hands.

Learn to Burn can be viewed as a wholly individual book in its own right, or as the smaller and cuter sibling of *Woodburning with Style*. This book is a selection of new projects aimed at the apprentice pyrographer wishing to practice his own skills by following step-by-step guides, while building up the confidence to start designing his own creations. The projects are based on and influenced by my own personal *Wood Tattoos* style of woodburning, featuring bold patterns, subtle texture, and alternate sources of inspiration. While my first book was an in-depth guide to pyrography, covering all topics from start to finish, this book is aimed to be quick, punchy, and direct, and perfectly suited for the beginner. The projects are designed to be easy to follow so that you can pick up the book, complete the steps, create your own items, and be left wanting to burn some more!

The project instructions can be followed to the letter while you develop your own pyrography skills, and you can adapt them to suit your own style and personal preferences when you feel more confident in your skills. Many of the projects feature tips and pointers introducing other avenues you may wish to explore. The final chapter contains a selection of patterns and designs that can be used to vary your project designs, as well as a small gallery of some of my creations to show you where I have gone creatively with certain ideas or themes.

If you've read this and are now ready for some pyrography, what are you waiting for? Ready... steady... burn!

Chapter 1:

Getting Started

This book has been designed as a practical guide to pyrography through the use of step-by-step projects, allowing budding pyrographers to hone their skills in a hands-on fashion. Each project has been designed to allow the reader to quickly pick up the requirements of the project in a visual manner, with photographic illustrations and clear, concise captions. This first chapter contains a basic introduction to the art of pyrography for those crafters who are experiencing it for the first time. The chapter contains an introduction to pyrography machines and the correct way to use them, as well as available accessories, basic mark making, selecting woods, and finishing techniques. There are a number of brief exercises to help beginners gain experience using a pyrography machine before moving on to the projects. If you would like to examine this area more fully, my first book, *Woodburning with Style*, contains a more detailed introduction to the art of pyrography.

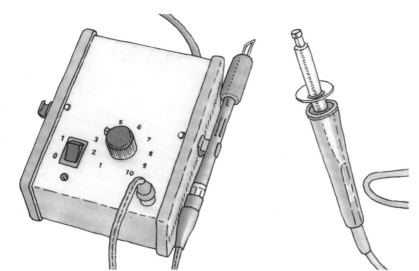

Hot wire machines (left) generally have a transformer unit, while solid point machines (right) usually resemble a soldering iron.

Hold your pyrography pen in the same way you would hold a pen or pencil, so that the movement feels natural when you burn.

ANATOMY OF A PYROGRAPHY MACHINE

The term pyrography is derived from words that mean "writing with fire" or "writing with heat," and the primary feature that all pyrography machines have in common is the ability to generate heat in order to make marks on a surface. Modern pyrography machines are available in two basic types: solid point machines and hot wire machines.

Solid point machines resemble a soldering iron in appearance, consisting of a chunky pen (containing the heating element) with an electric flex leading directly from the base. The tips are made of solid metal and can be purchased in a variety of shapes to make different lines and marks. Solid point pyrography machines tend to be the cheapest in price.

Hot wire machines are generally more expensive than solid point machines, but are usually considered more versatile than their solid point counterparts. They are made up of a transformer unit (which is plugged into the mains) attached to a pen by a separate cable. This means the pen itself is often smaller and easier to handle than that of a solid point machine. The main unit usually has a variable temperature gauge so the pen can be used at a wide range of heat settings to suit different surface materials or create different qualities of lines and marks. The pens are also available with a range of differently shaped nibs or wires.

Like many pyrographers, I prefer using a hot wire machine. They are generally easier to handle in terms of size and weight, and quicker to heat up and cool down than solid point machines. At the end of the day, the pyrography machine you use is all about personal preference, so it is best to try a machine, if at all possible, before you buy it.

HOLDING A PYROGRAPHY PEN

Creating a design using pyrography means you need to hold the pen for considerable periods of time as you work. It is therefore vitally important that you feel comfortable while holding and using the pen. Think about the type of pen you prefer to use when writing normally: do you prefer using a slim, lightweight pen, or one that is thicker and has more weight? Considering these factors will help you select a pyrography machine that is most suited to your needs.

A pyrography pen is basically held in the same way as a normal writing pen or pencil, but you will have to consider the heat it produces. Position your fingers far enough from the heated end to avoid any pain or discomfort, but close enough that you do not feel you are struggling to control the nib as you work. Many pens have some form of protection to prevent injury, such as foam insulation grips or a shaped finger guard. These protective elements can help you get a good, comfortable grip on your pen.

If you are able to, it is well worth handling a pyrography pen before making a purchase, whether at a store or using one borrowed from a friend. The last thing you want to do is make a substantial financial purchase and find that you are not comfortable using the machine. It is essential for the pyrography pen to feel like a natural extension of your hand as you work. Any awkwardness or discomfort will come across in your designs, so spend time making sure you buy the equipment that best suits you.

Keep your fingers as far as possible from the hot nib while burning. In this photo, you may be able to see the small burn on my left forefinger from a time when I forgot this rule!

GENERAL SAFETY

The most important thing to remember when using a pyrography machine is the heat generated by it while it is in use. A tip does not have to be glowing red to be hot, and it is important to take every precaution when handling the nib. Always err on the side of caution and treat it as if it is hot. It is useful to keep a piece of scrap paper to one side as you work so you can press the nib lightly against it in order to see if the paper burns or shows signs of darkening from the heat of the nib.

Do not attempt to change nibs while the previous one is still potentially hot. If you find you're impatient, take a break for a few minutes, and walk away if necessary to allow plenty of time for the pen to cool down. The same applies if the handle of your pen starts to feel hot after an extended period of burning. Turn it off and let it cool down completely before starting to work again.

Do not place your pen down in an unsecured position while it is still on. If you need to put your pen down in the middle of burning and don't want to turn it off, use some form of pen rest made from a suitable material. Many hot wire machines have a shaped pen grip or hook on the side of the main unit for this purpose. Otherwise, turn off your pen and allow it to cool down before setting it down or storing it.

Work in a well-ventilated area whenever possible. Burning wood and other materials creates smoke and fumes that can be harmful if inhaled. Setting up an electric fan pointing away from your work is a useful way of drawing any smoke away from your work area without cooling the heated element of the pen. Alternatively, consider wearing goggles or a mask if you plan to work on a substantial project for long periods.

In addition to being well-ventilated, your pyrography workspace should also be well-lit and free of clutter.

Tidy your workspace regularly to remove any scraps of paper, bits of masking tape, or other items you are not using for your current project so they do not get in the way while you burn. I recommend placing some form of protective mat over your worktable or desk to keep it from being burned. A piece of scrap wood or sturdy hardboard are suitable low-cost alternatives to the protective mats sold in craft supply stores.

Keep pyrography machines away from children at all times, and do not work near chemicals, flammable substances, or other potentially flammable items. Be careful to ensure the wires of the machine do not become twisted or end up near to the nib of the pen while you are working. This may inhibit your movement as you burn and could result in damage to your equipment. If the cord becomes tangled, turn the machine off, allow the pen to cool, and take time to untangle all the wires separately before you start burning again.

Make sure you keep your fingers as far as possible from the area you are burning, particularly when working on small or unusually shaped items. Do not work in a position that makes you feel uncomfortable, as this may cause your hands to grow sore or painful over time. Take regular breaks if burning for long periods to rest your hands and prevent any aches and pains from building up.

Do not use your pyrography machine if you believe it is damaged in any way. Be alert for any possible signs of damage (such as sparks, buzzing noises, or cracked components) and take your equipment to be checked over by a qualified electrician if you have any concerns about it.

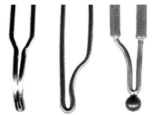

Writing nibs come in different shapes and sizes, but they can all be used for the same purpose. Spoon point nibs have a spoon-like shape and can be used for shading or to make lines.

BASIC TIPS AND THEIR MARKS

The range of shaped nibs and tips available for both solid point and hot wire machines is quite simply staggering. Many companies have created an extensive range of tips that can be purchased as accessories to their basic woodburning kit, each nib aimed at producing a particular style or type of mark. I've experimented with various nibs during my time as a pyrographer and found there are certain types that are essential, due to their versatility, while other, more specialized, nibs are perfect for certain marks, but not vital in the long run. At the end of the day, the types and number of nibs or tips you choose to use comes down to your own personal preference and budget.

I have a wide selection of nibs, but there are a handful that I use much more frequently than others. I believe there are four nib types that are essential staples for any pyrographer. With these four nibs alone, you can create an array of lines and marks that cover a range of purposes and situations.

My first essential nib is a general writing nib. These have a simple bent or rounded tip, making them very versatile across a wooden surface. They can be moved around smoothly in any number of ways, without catching or snagging, to create straight or irregular lines, as well as spirals, curves, dots, and text.

The spoon point nib is probably my favorite nib and the one I use most frequently because of its versatility. As the name suggests, these nibs are bowl-shaped and can be used in a number of ways depending on the angle at which you hold them. The soft underside of the bowl can be used for soft shading and filling in areas of tone, while the thin edge of the spoon is great for making linear marks, cross-hatching, or patterned shading. I have created many designs with a spoon point nib alone, due to its wide range of uses.

Shading nibs are available in a range of shapes and sizes, but they all share a wide profile. The enlarged surface area of these nibs enables them to shade more quickly and efficiently than a nib with a sharp point due to the increased amount of metal in contact with the surface being burned. Shading nibs are available in a range of sizes and shapes, including spears, chisels, circles, spades, or coils. The shape you select will depend on your personal preference. Some specialized

Writing nibs can be used to make a variety of marks, from clear, straight lines to textures. Here are just some of the things you can do with a writing nib.

You can use different parts of a spoon point nib to create a variety of marks. The underside of the nib is perfect for shading, while the edge can be used to make clean lines.

Shading nibs have a large surface area, making them perfect for quickly shading areas of your projects.

Bladed nibs have a sharp edge that cuts into the surface of the item you are burning.

shading tips are designed to produce textured shading to create marks mimicking fur or feathers.

My final essential nib is a blade point or skew nib. These nibs have a sharply defined straight edge and are similar in appearance to a scalpel. Their shape makes these nibs ideal for crisp lines and textures, as the blade cuts into the surface of the item you are burning, allowing it to run in a neat, sharp line rather than skipping across the surface or snagging on the texture of the grain. These nibs are perfect for detailed work, such as outlines, fine texture, and lettering.

All of the projects featured in this book can be created using these four essential nib types. If you are just starting out in pyrography, I recommend purchasing these four nibs to get yourself started, and then add to your collection as you gain experience. I should note that most nib types are versatile and can be used for more than one purpose. As you gain experience and start to build your own individual style, you can branch out and explore how other nibs can add something different to your mark-making palette and experiment with different ways to use them.

As with any artistic medium, it is important to spend time experimenting with the tools you have purchased and to see what you can do with them. Find some scrap pieces of wood and spend time with each nib to discover what happens when you try out different angles and methods of applying it to the wood's surface. Vary the temperature settings on your pyrography machine, length of time you hold the nib against the wood, and so on. By doing this, you can create a visual scrapbook for future reference to help you remember how you created a specific mark.

For the more adventurous pyrographer, some pyrography machine manufacturers sell pens with holding posts that can be used to hold custom-shaped nibs made from Nichrome wire. These custom nibs are held to the holding posts with small screws or a similar object. You can experiment with creating your own nibs by bending Nichrome wire into various shapes, working to increase or decrease the working surface area of the nib, as well as shaping it with needle files or other tools to fit your specific needs.

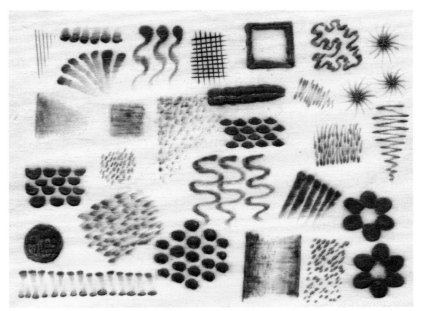

Shading nibs are best used for making marks such as these.

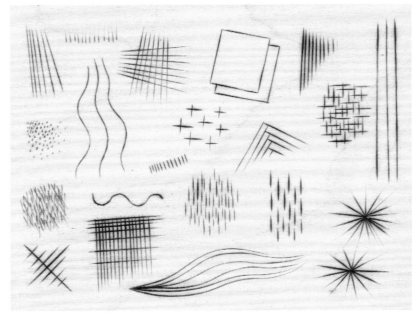

Because of their edges, bladed nibs are perfect for fine detail work and creating sharp lines.

SELECTING WOOD

Selecting the appropriate wood is a vital part of creating a successful pyrography design. The best woods to use for pyrography are pale in color with a fine grain, because this allows for strong contrast and smooth shading. Beech and sycamore are good examples of wood with these qualities, but there are many other species suitable for pyrography, including maple, holly, lime, oak, and more.

It is important to remember that wood is a natural material, having once formed part of a living tree. As a result, many wooden blanks or pieces will feature natural markings and blemishes that add to the

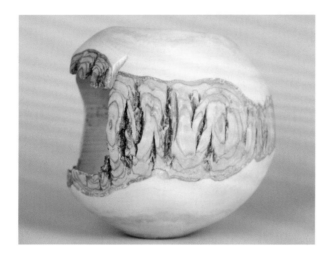

Wood is a natural material, and your designs should make the most of the beautiful and unique canvas it provides.

character and personality of the final project. Sensitive application of a design to a wood piece can enhance the natural beauty of the wood by emphasizing or incorporating the grain, knots, or other markings.

Woods with a strong grain can cause the pyrography pen to snag on the wood surface, producing poor or irregular lines. Soft or sappy woods, on the other hand, can burn too easily and clog up the nib, causing problems if the design you are trying to create contains fine detail.

Medium-density fiberboard (MDF) and similar composite materials should *not* be used for pyrography under any circumstances. The wooden elements in these materials are held together with strong glues and chemicals that give off harmful toxic fumes when burned.

There is an array of wooden blanks available designed specifically for pyrography, including boxes, signs, plates, plaques, fobs, household items, toys, and more. The projects contained here were all designed to use these readymade items, which are available at your local craft store or from online suppliers.

In addition to wood, you can burn a number of other materials with a pyrography machine. Leather is a popular choice for many pyrographers, who create designs on vegetable-tanned leather, which is safe to burn into with pleasing results. Pyrography can also be applied to materials like paper, card stock, cork, or gourds. The projects in this book all focus on wooden blanks, but you will be able to try other materials as your desire to experiment as your new skill develops.

FINISHING TECHNIQUES

Once you have successfully added a pyrography design to a wood item, it is only natural that you would wish to protect the item to keep it looking its best. Wood can be enhanced by a range of finishing treatments, including oils and varnishes. Whatever treatment you wish to use, it is best to test a sample of the finish on a scrap piece of wood first to prevent inadvertently ruining all the hard work you have done by choosing a finish that ruins or obscures your pyrography marks.

Danish oil is my preferred finishing treatment for most of my pyrography projects. It gives the finished piece a warm luster that enhances the wood and the contrast between the surface and the pyrography design. Danish oil can be applied using a soft cloth or tissue and should then be set aside to dry in a well-ventilated area.

Clear varnishes can be applied to wooden items that would benefit from greater surface protection. These varnishes are generally available in a range of finishes, including satin, matte, or gloss. Consider applying a varnish if you know your finished item will likely be handled frequently, because the coating will protect the wood from the natural oils on your hands.

The keyring fob on the right has been treated with Danish oil, giving it a warm appearance when compared to the untreated blank on the left.

Pyrography marks fade with time if exposed to strong sunlight, so it is not always a suitable method of decoration for items intended for outdoor use. If you are working on a design to be displayed outside, consider placing it in a well-shaded area and coating it with a hardwearing finish, such as yacht varnish (also known as marine/spar varnish). Finishes like this often contain UV inhibitors to protect the surface of your project from the effects of sustained sunlight exposure. For best protection, you should recoat the piece every two to three years.

Remember to follow the manufacturer's instructions for any oils or treatments that you use, particularly in regard to storage, ventilation, and recommended drying times between coats or applications.

Consider when you would need to apply a finish to your pieces. Bear in mind that items will need time to dry fully if an oil or similar type of finish is applied before they can be placed on a wall or tablecloth, as the oil might seep into the other surface. If you are using paints or inks in a design, you may also want to experiment with the finish you wish to use beforehand to make sure the color of your paint does not bleed or dilute once the treatment is applied.

EXERCISE 1: GETTING TO KNOW YOUR PYROGRAPHY MACHINE

The steps in this exercise are designed to help you get acquainted with your new pyrography machine. Some of the tasks may not be relevant to certain machine types, so please feel free to pick and choose whatever helps you. If you cannot adjust the temperature on your particular machine, for example, just skip to the next step or exercise.

Power supply. Follow the manufacturer's instructions for plugging your machine into your power supply. Check that the cord is long enough for you to work safely and comfortably at your workspace. If necessary, use an extension cord to reach the length you need. Check the cord for damage and make sure it is not loose. Make sure the cord is not twisted, stretched, or obstructing your working area in any way.

Fitting the nibs. If your machine has a range of nibs or tips, practice fitting and changing them. Make sure your machine is not turned on inadvertently before doing this. Check that each nib fits securely in the machine for a good connection, as a poor connection can affect the consistency of any burning you do.

Holding the pen. Try holding the pyrography pen to see which position feels the most comfortable. Treat it like a regular writing pen in the way that you hold and move it. Experiment with the position of your fingers for maximum control. Ensure that you make use of any protective features to keep your fingers away from the heated nib.

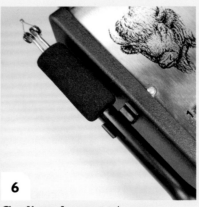

Turning on your machine. Make sure the nib is not touching anything before you turn your machine on. Take extra care if the machine does not have a separate power switch and needs to be turned on at the electrical outlet. Some machines have a hook to hold the pen safely while not in use. If your machine doesn't have one, you may be able to buy or make a separate rest for it.

Adjusting the temperature. Once the pen has been turned on, experiment with the temperature settings (if your machine has this capability). Look at the nib for any change in color or appearance as you adjust the temperature up and down. Test the nib by pressing it against a scrap piece of wood each time you adjust the heat so you can see the results.

Cooling down. Make sure you are aware where the heated nib is before you turn off your machine. Place the pen on a hook or rest if you have one. Turn the machine off and allow plenty of time for the nib to cool. Experiment by pressing the nib against a scrap piece of wood or heavy cardstock every few minutes after the machine's been turned off to see how long it takes to cool down completely.

EXERCISE 2: MAKING SIMPLE LINES AND MARKS

Learning how to make marks on a surface with your pyrography machine is ultimately the most important skill you will need. Start by experimenting on scrap pieces of wood, making notes next to each set of marks for reference. You can then build up a visual sourcebook of different lines and marks to help you with future projects.

1

Experiment with your first marks. Secure a writing tip to your pen and set your machine to a medium temperature setting (if the temperature can be adjusted). Start by scribbling random marks onto the surface of a piece of scrap wood. Check that you are comfortable using the pen and observe the different marks you can make on the wood.

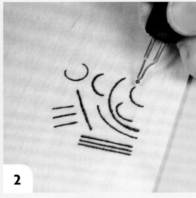

2

Practice making curved and straight lines. Move on to creating more structured lines and marks. Use the writing nib to create both straight and curved lines on the wood, repeating the marks as many times as you need to feel satisfied with the results. Your goal should be lines that are as smooth and even as possible. Notice how the surface of the wood can both assist and hinder this objective at times.

3

Practice changing direction. Once you are happy with the results of the previous step, move on to creating lines that require a change of angle or direction, and combinations of lines that join together. Try to make the angles and connections between your lines as tidy as you can. The ability to change direction and angle and connect lines will allow you to work in corners and other tight spaces or create longer lines.

4

Adjust your speed. Continue making marks like those described in the previous step, but alter the speed at which you move the nib across the wood and the amount of time you leave the nib in contact with the wood. Quickly made marks can give exciting, spontaneous results, while marks made more slowly can lend solidity to a line. Look at how the marks you have created differ from your earlier attempts.

5

Adjust the temperature. Repeat steps 1–3 again, but experiment with the temperature setting on your pyrography machine (if possible). Observe how the marks look different when created with a nib at a high temperature setting compared to those made at a much lower temperature. See if the temperature setting makes certain marks easier to create or provides a different final result.

6

Experiment with other nibs. Repeat the previous steps with all the nibs on your pyrography machine. Every nib has its own strengths, so learn what these are and how to use them by testing the nibs as many times and in as many ways as you can. You will find the potential results are almost limitless.

EXERCISE 3: SIMPLE SHADING TECHNIQUES

In this exercise, you will start to combine lines and marks to form areas of tone and shading. By practicing these techniques, you will build up your skills and confidence in creating a range of even tones from dark to light. You will also work on completing sections of graduated tone, which show a transition from dark to light and vice versa.

1

Create a dark tone. Use a broad shading nib at a medium/high temperature setting to create an area of solid, even, dark tone on a piece of scrap wood. Work over the surface a number of times until you are happy with the quality of the shading. Observe the way changes or features in the wood's surface can affect your ability to shade evenly.

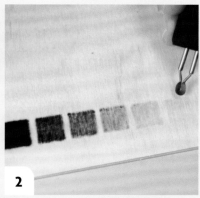

2

Create a series of lighter tones. Working with the same nib, create a series of shaded areas, each with a slightly lighter tone than the last. Try to make the color of the tone as even as you can. Experiment with using lower temperatures to help you. You can also reduce the amount of time you keep the nib against the wood or the number of times you work back over the shading to achieve gradually lighter results.

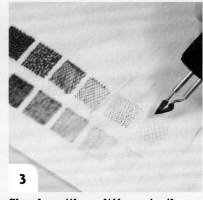

3

Shade with a different nib. Experiment with other nibs to create tones and shading through the use of other combined marks and lines. You might try cross-hatching (arranging lines in a criss-cross pattern) and stippling (closely arranging dots). See how the tone changes when you start to increase the distance between such lines or dots or change the tone of the mark itself.

4

Create a graduated tone. Attach a broad shading nib to your pen and set your machine to a low temperature setting. Create a large strip of light tone. Rework the shading at one end of the strip, gradually making it darker as you move toward the other end. Repeat this process several times, slowly and steadily working from one end of the strip to the other, making each section a little darker than the last.

5

Finish the gradation. Keep working your way along the strip until you are making a very small section of dark tone at the opposite end from where you started. The end goal is a section of tone that shows a smooth transition from light to dark. You may find you need to rework areas of the shading if the result is not smooth in places. Any areas like this might be caused by changes in the surface of the wood.

6

Practice gradation using other techniques. Experiment with other ways to create gradual changes in tone and shade using different nibs or techniques as in Step 3. You can create gradual stippling tones easily, for example, by changing the density and spread of the dots over an area, or by using a combination of dots that gradually get darker or bigger. Have fun and see what you can achieve!

Chapter 2:

Pyrography Projects

This chapter contains fourteen projects using a range of different blanks and materials, all of which should be easily available through your local craft store, online suppliers, or friendly craftspeople! The first nine projects involve simple designs on small items to allow you to practice and build up your skills, while the final five feature more complex designs. Each project starts with a brief introduction, including a list of the tools and materials you will need. If desired, you can follow each project's step-by-step instructions to the letter, which will guide you in creating your own replica of the featured object. You can also choose to tailor each item to suit your individual preferences, using the principles of each project as an informal guide rather than a rigid set of rules. The five final projects also contain tips and advice on developing the featured designs into more personal projects that express your own creative ideas. The patterns for each project can be found in Chapter 3.

Tools and Materials

- Several wooden napkin ring blanks

- Pencil and eraser

- Tracing paper

- Scissors, craft knife, or scalpel

- Masking tape

- Ruler

- Pyrography machine

- Spear nib

- Spoon point nib

- Shading nib

NAPKIN RINGS

Patterns on pages 67–68.

When you start making your own pyrography designs, the first thing you'll want to do is share them with friends and loved ones! Making napkin rings to decorate a dining table for a special occasion provides an ideal platform to display your newfound creative talents. You can personalize the napkin rings with names or decorations to suit the occasion. The napkin rings can act as place cards to guide guests to their allocated seats, and are perfect gifts for each guest to take home and keep as a memento of the celebration.

Napkin rings are an ideal choice for your first pyrography project. They are inexpensive and readily available in large quantities from a range of craft suppliers. They provide a good opportunity for you to practice detailed work on a challenging surface, due

to the small size and curved form. In addition, they are often made in a range of styles and appearances, from modern, contemporary designs, which may be simple and geometric in appearance, to more ornate and traditional forms with shaped edges and surfaces. You will be able to tailor your decoration to suit the blanks you have purchased, or buy a specific style of napkin ring to suit the creative ideas you have in mind.

For this project, you will create a selection of napkin rings designed for a wedding, with decorations based on the role of each guest. You can easily apply the same principle to napkin rings for any other occasion you are organizing or attending. This first project is aimed at helping you build your control of the pyrography pen while burning lettering and intricate designs.

1

Trace the lettering. Cut pieces of tracing paper to fit the width and circumference of your napkin rings. Then, trace the lettering for your napkin rings onto it with a pencil. You can freehand the lettering or use your computer to print out the lettering in a font you like. I chose to use the Lucida Calligraphy font available on my computer.

2

Transfer the lettering. Secure the traced lettering onto each napkin ring blank with masking tape. Use a pencil to transfer the lettering onto the wooden surface by scribbling on the reverse side. Note: Adjusting the size of the lettering and mirroring it before printing shortens the transfer process

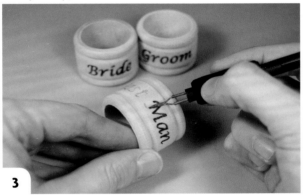

3

Burn the lettering. Using a spear point nib on a medium temperature setting, fill in the lettering outline carefully on each napkin ring. Be careful of your finger position while working. This project will definitely help to increase your control of the pen as you burn!

4

Trace and transfer the design. Measure the space left on the napkin rings between the last and first letters. Trace the required size of your chosen design onto the tracing paper, cut it out, and secure it to the napkin rings with masking tape. Then, transfer the design onto your napkin rings as before.

5

Burn the design. Use a spoon point nib on a medium temperature setting to block in the design on each napkin ring with a shaded tone. Using the narrow lip of the spoon will help you make flowing lines along the edges, while using the bowl of the nib will help you shade the areas between the outlines more easily.

6

Add decorative edging. Use a shading nib on a high temperature setting to create decorative edging on each napkin ring. Press the face of the nib into the wood at regular intervals, working around the rim of the blank to create a repeated pattern from the shape of the nib itself. Different nibs allow you to create different patterns.

25

Tools and Materials

- Several blank wooden gift tags
- Pencil
- Eraser
- Tracing paper (optional)
- Masking tape (optional)
- Scissors, craft knife, or scalpel
- Pyrography machine
- Spear nib
- Bladed nib
- Spoon point nib
- Lengths of decorative ribbon, string, or cord

GIFT TAGS

Patterns on page 69.

Wooden gift tags are a great item to burn on when you are new to pyrography. They are readily available from most crafts suppliers in a range of shapes and sizes. They can often be purchased with pre-drilled holes so they can be attached to a present with string or ribbon, but it is not difficult to drill your own holes with a small hand drill if required. The tags are often made of birch plywood, giving you a pale, smooth surface on which to work. You may also be able to find suppliers who sell tags made from solid woods.

In addition to the usual geometric shapes, you can often purchase tags shaped for a range of special occasions or seasons, such as snowflakes, stars, animals, hearts, and more. These specialized tags add the perfect personal touch to birthday, Christmas, Valentine's Day,

and anniversary gifts. With such a wide range of shaped blanks available for purchase, it is easy to find a tag that suits the recipient's likes, hobbies, or personality. When the recipient realizes you made something unique for him, he may choose to find another use for the special gift tag, like as a keyring decoration, Christmas ornament, or other keepsake.

You can also add a personal message for the recipient to your tag, allowing you the opportunity to practice your pyrography pen control while creating text. A handmade gift tag can be just as meaningful as the gift itself. This project uses a Christmas theme for inspiration, but you can easily design your own gift tags for any special occasion by choosing suitable images or patterns.

1

Sketch the text. Draw the lettering for the gift tag's greeting message on one side of the wooden tag. If you are not happy with your own handwriting, consider using a simple computer font to prepare the text, and then transfer it to the wood with tracing paper.

2

Sketch the design. Turn the gift tag blank over and draw the outline of your decorative design onto the other side. You can trace and transfer a design if you do not like drawing freehand. Transferring designs can also save time if you are repeating a design on several gift tags.

3

Burn the text. Flip the tag back over and burn the lettering by using a spear point nib and a medium temperature setting. Move the point of the nib slowly and steadily across the surface of the wood to create a line that is as smooth and even as possible.

4

Burn the design outline. Flip the tag over again and burn the outline of your decorative design using a bladed nib and a medium temperature setting to create sharp, crisp lines. Move the tag whenever necessary to let your hand draw the line in a natural position rather than twisting your wrist. Try to make each line meet as neatly as you can.

5

Shade the design. Complete the shading on the design using a spoon point nib. Experiment with different temperature settings to create darker and lighter tones (working slowly or quickly over the surface will also change the tone). Add linear detail using the lip rather than the bowl of the spoon point nib.

6

Burn a border. Use a spear point nib on a high temperature setting to create a decorative scalloped border pattern along the edges on both sides of the tag. Change the pattern by varying the spacing between each mark or the angle and length of the nib you press into the wood.

Tools and Materials

- Several wooden key fob blanks with accompanying metal split rings

- Pencil and eraser

- Tracing paper

- Masking tape

- Scissors, craft knife, or scalpel

- Pyrography machine

- Spear nib

- Bladed nib

- Spoon point nib

KEY FOBS

Patterns on page 71.

Keys are an essential part of our day-to-day life, whether they belong to a home, a car, the office, a locker, or a storage box. Key fobs are the perfect way to make a set of keys more readily identifiable or personal. If you have several sets of keys, a key fob may be a good way of distinguishing them so you can more easily find the particular set for which you are looking. Key fobs also make nice gifts and can be designed to incorporate a decorative element that appeals to the recipient.

Key fobs are readily available as wooden blanks from most good crafts suppliers. They are relatively cheap to purchase, and a metal split ring is often included, making them very affordable. Because they are quite small, they can be worked on and completed in a short period of time. The design for your key fob can be as simple or as complicated as you wish. Despite their small size, a well-executed design can give them a jewel-like quality, making them a pleasure to look at and handle.

For this project, you will make a personalized key fob using decorative letters or initials, allowing you to create a customized present for a family member or friend. There are countless fonts you can use for the lettering. I chose to freehand a traditional calligraphy font because of the decorative quality of such an ornate alphabet. You can find examples of such lettering in books on calligraphy, online, or as part of the fonts available on your home computer.

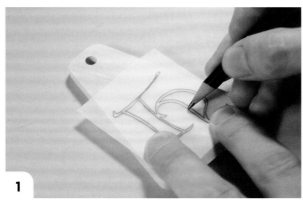

1

Transfer the lettering. Select the lettering or design you'd like to add to your key fob. Use a computer or photocopier to make it the correct size. Then, trace your chosen design or letter onto a piece of tracing paper cut to the size of your key fob. Position the tracing paper on the wooden key fob blank and transfer the outline from the reverse side.

2

Outline the design. Use a bladed nib at a medium temperature setting to burn the outline of the letter or design. Try to create smooth, fluid lines, taking care not to twist or snag the nib in the wood's surface. Adjust the fob's position regularly so your hand can move freely in the required direction.

3

Fill in the design. Use a spoon point nib on a medium/high setting to fill in the areas between the lines you created with the bladed nib. Take care not to burn over the lines. Use the very tip of the bowl and move away from the lines into the area between them to prevent any mistakes.

4

Add shading. Create a graduated tone to fill in the rest of the design, using a spoon point nib on a low/medium setting. Build up the shading slowly by going over and over the areas at the darker end of the tone. You will probably only have to pass over the lightest end one or two times, while the darker end will need more coverage.

5

Transfer a second outline. Transfer the outline of your design onto the fob again, offsetting it against the original design to create a shadow. Positioning the outline slightly lower and to the left of the original design creates the desired effect. Transfer the outline onto the wood in the areas where it can be seen around the original design.

6

Burn the shadow. Use a spear point nib on a medium/high setting to fill in the shadow by stippling it (adding repeated small dots close together the achieve the desired tone). Once you have filled in the shadow, use an eraser to remove any pencil lines that are still visible before fitting the metal split ring through the hole of the fob blank.

Tools and Materials

- Several small, shaped wooden blanks or tiles

- Pencil and eraser

- Tracing paper

- Masking tape

- Scissors, craft knife, or scalpel

- Several small craft magnets

- Super glue (if required)

- Pyrography machine

- Spear nib

- Bladed nib

- Spoon point nib

FRIDGE MAGNETS

Patterns on pages 72.

The fridge can often be regarded as the communication center of our family! The door is regularly covered in school letters, shopping lists, photos, drawings, receipts, and much more. Each of these is held on by an assortment of magnets, usually from my daughter's play sets or purchased as mementoes from places we have visited. This project is aimed at helping you produce decorative magnets that can lend some order to the chaos of the average fridge door!

Making fridge magnets using pyrography is another fun and inexpensive project. You can use almost any wooden blank available, as long as it's light enough to be held to the door with your magnet. Magnets for this project can be bought from all reliable arts and crafts stores. They often have adhesive backs, allowing you to stick them directly to projects. If your magnets don't

have adhesive backs, you can glue them in place with super glue.

The objective of this project is to create a set of magnets that are both fun and functional. I decorated each of my magnets as a chess piece, so my family could play a game of chess while we went about our daily routine. You can create your own magnet chess set, or, if you don't play chess, you can apply the same principle to make your own board game magnets. Make a game board for your magnets by drawing or printing the board's design onto paper and attaching it to the fridge door. Alternatively, make the individual board squares from adhesive vinyl sheets, available at most art and craft stores. You can also make alphabet magnets to help your children with their spelling, or why not try making a jigsaw by burning a large image across several wooden blanks?

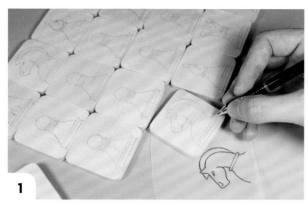

1

Transfer the designs. Draw or trace your designs onto the center of each blank with a pencil. Make sure you make the correct number of each playing piece (for a chess set: two kings, two queens, four bishops, and so on). If you're drawing your designs freehand, draw one design, and then trace it and transfer it to the other tiles to make them identical.

2

Burn the outlines. Use a bladed nib on a medium setting to burn the outlines of each piece in turn. Take care when burning curves, taking the time to make the lines as neat and smooth as possible. Erase any remaining visible pencil lines once the outline for each piece has been completed.

3

Begin shading the black pieces. Use a spoon point nib on a high setting to shade the darkest areas of the black pieces. Imagine that the pieces are three-dimensional, and think how the light would fall across each one. With this in mind, add the darkest shading to areas where the light source would not illuminate the playing piece.

4

Finish shading the black pieces. Continue using the spoon point nib at a high setting to shade the remaining areas of the black pieces with a stippling effect to enhance the three-dimensional look. Some areas of detail can be left unshaded for contrast, such as the cross on the king's crown and the door of the castle/rook.

5

Shade the white pieces. Using a spear nib on a medium/high setting, create the same three-dimensional effect you made on the black pieces on the white pieces with stippled shading. Use a dense concentration of dots for the darkest areas, and then fade the dots out gradually as you work toward the areas of light.

6

Finish the magnets. Finish each piece with any desired detail or contrast, such as using subtle lines on the castle/rook to create a brickwork effect. Use white detail on the black chess pieces, such as the king and the queen, and black detail on the white pieces. Secure magnets to the back of each blank, using super glue if necessary.

Learn to Burn

Tools and Materials

- Several shaped wooden coaster blanks

- Pencil and eraser

- Ruler

- Compass or circle stencil

- Pyrography machine

- Spear nib

- Spoon point nib

- Tracing paper (optional)

- Masking tape (optional)

- Scissors, craft knife, or scalpel (optional)

TABLE COASTERS

Patterns on pages 73–74.

Coaster blanks are extremely easy to find and are often available in a range of shapes and sizes. Their flat surface makes them perfect items for beginners to practice burning on, while their small size makes burning a coaster set an unintimidating, perfectly achievable project! Because coaster sets usually contain multiple coasters with the same pattern, this project is a perfect opportunity for new pyrographers to practice recreating identical designs on several items. Making your own coaster set allows you to create the exact number and style of pieces you need, rather than trying to find the right style to fit your taste at a home goods store. Coasters can be personalized for each family member, office colleague, place setting at your table, and so on.

You can also increase the scale of your coaster designs to create larger coasters or placemats to form a matching set for your dining table. By customizing your

own designs, you can create your very own unique and decorative eating area. Most standard coaster blanks are available in birch plywood, beech, or sycamore. You may wish to look into buying more specialized wood blanks if there is a certain color or finish you want.

Texture and pattern have always been important recurring features in my design work, regardless of the medium or materials I've used. Pyrography lends itself well to such decorative styles, as the marks burned into the wood can work in combination with the natural appearance of the wood with stunning results. This project illustrates the use of a rippled circular pattern. Several other design suggestions are available for you in Chapter 3, or you may also be inspired to create your own design based on patterns and textures you encounter where you live.

1

Draw a border. Use a ruler and pencil to draw a border line ⅜" (10mm) from the edge of each side of the coaster blanks. This creates an area to contain your design's texture. As you can see on the finished coasters, I did not burn this border. It is not always necessary to create a physical border with solid lines. Just the visual effect of a virtual border can be very pleasing.

2

Draw or transfer your design. Draw or transfer your design to the area inside the coaster's border. For my design, I added a number of 3⁄16" (5mm) circles in random positions. To follow my design, add five to ten of these circles to each coaster. Make the coasters different by experimenting with the distance between each circle to add spontaneity, variety, and interest to your design.

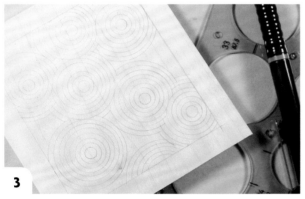

3

Outline the circles. Use your compass or circle template to build up a series of concentric rings around the original 3⁄16" (5mm) circles. Each new circle should be ⅛" (4mm) larger in diameter than the last one, and should be centered as best as possible over the previous circle. As your circles become larger, they will run into each other. Stop drawing a line when it meets another drawn circle.

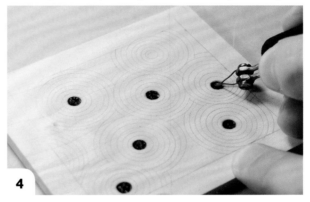

4

Fill in the smallest circles. Use your spoon point nib on a medium/high setting to shade each 3⁄16" (5mm) circle with a solid dark tone. Keep the shading as neat as possible to maintain the smooth circular shape, trying not to cross over the pencil outline of the circles.

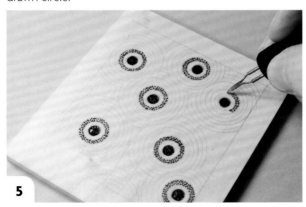

5

Shade the next ring. Change to a spear nib on a high setting. Leave the rings adjacent to your shaded circles blank, and shade the next rings with a dense stippled pattern. Keep within the pencil lines as best you can to keep the circular rings smooth and regular.

6

Finish shading the circles. Continue working outward, applying stippled shading to every other ring. The shading in some of the outermost rings will connect where the rings meet. Do not add shading outside the border lines you drew in Step 1 so you maintain a virtual border around the square of texture in the center of the coasters. Erase any pencil lines when finished.

- Shaped wooden key holder or plaque blank
- Several metal/wooden hooks or pegs
- Hand drill and bit (if your blank is not pre-drilled)
- Wood glue (if using wooden pegs)
- Pencil and eraser
- Ruler
- Circle stencil or compass
- Tracing paper
- Masking tape
- Scissors, craft knife, or scalpel
- Pyrography machine
- Spear nib
- Bladed nib
- Spoon point nib

KEY HOLDER

Patterns on pages 75–76.

As mentioned in the introduction to the key fob project, we all use keys on a daily basis, and it's quite easy to misplace a set of keys as we go about our daily routine! Having a certain place to keep your keys is an ideal way of reducing the number of times you lose them. A key holder is also the perfect place to safely store keys you don't need to carry every day—like keys for a shed, garage, outhouse, holiday home, or other similar location.

Key holders make excellent gifts because they can be personalized to suit the style and character of the home where they will be displayed. The main body of a key holder is usually a solid wood plaque, available for purchase in a variety of shapes and sizes. Many plaques have shaped or decorative edges to make them more appealing. The key holder pegs themselves can come

in a variety of styles as well, from a shaped metal hook to more traditional wooden pegs. You can buy holders with a single peg or several, depending on the design and purpose you have in mind for your key holder.

Designing an item in the style of a favorite artist, movement, or era can be very rewarding. The design I created for my key holder was made in the Art Deco style from the 1920s and 1930s, using my own interpretation of the visual characteristics to fit in with the shape of my blank. If you are starting out, try creating a key holder using this design or one of the alternative patterns featured in Chapter 3. Once you've had some practice, why not look to develop your own artistic designs based on your preferred artists, illustrators, or designers?

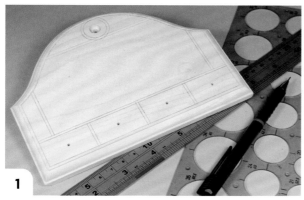

1

2

Create a border. Draw a pattern of border lines on your blank using a pencil, ruler, and circle template or compass. Use the shape and form of the blank to help you build a composition that fits the surface available. The border lines should be no more than 1⁄16"–1⁄8" (2–3mm) thick and should frame the blank's features, such as the hooks and screw hole.

Transfer or draw your design. Draw or transfer the central motif of the key holder to your blank. Use tracing paper if you want to replicate a design from the book, or draw your own design freehand if you prefer. The thickest lines of the motif should be no more than 1⁄32"–1⁄16" (1–2mm) thick. Use single lines for details such as the veins on leaves.

3

4

Burn the border and design outline. Use a bladed nib on a medium/high setting to burn all of the outlines of the border and motif design. Keep parallel lines as smooth and neat as possible to ensure the lines do not appear irregular once shaded. Erase any visible pencil marks once finished.

Fill in the outline. Carefully shade between the parallel border lines and the lines of the central motif using the edge of a spoon point nib on a medium/high setting to create even black lines. Try to keep within the lines you made during the previous step so the design remains crisp and sharp all over.

5

6

Add detail shading to the design. Turn your pyrography machine to a low/medium setting, and add detail shading with the spoon point nib. Dragging the bowl of the nib along the wood's surface, carefully lifting it off as you go, creates shading that gradually fades away. I used this method to shade the leaves of my design, working repeatedly from the center of each leaf. I also added some light shading along the lines of the flowers.

Add detail shading to the border. Finish the key holder using a spear nib on a medium/high setting to add soft stippled shading or subtle lines along the border lines. This adds a little depth to the border without drawing attention away from your central motif. Attach the hooks or pegs once the shading is complete.

Tools and Materials

- Shaped wooden bangle blank
- Pencil and eraser
- Ruler
- Tracing paper
- Masking tape
- Scissors, craft knife, or scalpel
- Pyrography machine
- Spear nib
- Spoon point nib
- Shading nib

BANGLE

Patterns on page 77.

The possibilities for decorative bangle designs are simply infinite. Adorning your body with jewelry is such a matter of personal taste that designing your own jewelry is often much easier than searching endlessly in a store for the perfect piece! Jewelry is a kind of temporary tattoo for the body. You can use jewelry to alter your appearance to fit a million different situations or occasions. This is why I enjoy making bangles that are rich in pattern and decoration.

Finding a supplier for wooden bangles can be tricky, as bangle blanks are not that common. There are several reliable online suppliers that will ship blanks internationally. Once you find the right supplier, you will see bangle blanks can be purchased in a range of sizes and shapes. You can find flat, curved, and shaped faces to work on, which can help inspire the design you

develop. It can be difficult to trace designs onto bangles with curved faces, so use them for freehand work as desired. You can draw your design onto them in pencil, or work directly on the blank with your pyrography machine. Be careful when burning on bangles: as with any small shaped item, it is easy to forget where your fingers are!

Everyone has a favorite line or quote from a song, poem, film, or book. Such literary references often form the basis for real tattoos, so using them to create a unique jewelry design for a loved one is an ideal alternative. The line I used for my bangle is from a poem I wrote for my wife on a very special occasion. You can find alternative quotes in Chapter 3, or you can select your own. My goal for this project was to create a bangle that looked like it was made from stone.

1

Trace or draw the text. Cut a piece of tracing paper to fit the width and circumference of your wooden bangle. Print or write your selected text at a size that will fit the tracing paper, and trace it onto the paper, drawing a border along each edge if desired. I used the Viner Hand ITC font available on my computer for my text.

2

Transfer the text. Attach the tracing paper to the bangle's surface securely with masking tape. Scribble on the reverse side of the tracing paper with a pencil to transfer the lettering onto the surface of the bangle, and then carefully remove the paper. I added a small hand-drawn element, a small crescent moon, to help separate the start and end of the quote.

3

Burn the lettering. Use a spear nib on a high temperature setting to burn the outline of the lettering and any additional elements. Work around the outside of each letter, leaving the letters themselves untouched but creating a dark outline. Work away from the lines of each letter, using random marks and scribbles to give a rough, chaotic appearance.

4

Burn the border lines. Use the bowl of a spoon point nib on a high temperature setting to create the same effect used for the lettering along the outside of each border line. Again, use loose, scribbled lines and marks to maintain the organic, rough texture across the surface.

5

Add texture. Use a large shading nib on a medium setting to create a rough texture around the letters and borders. You can do this in a number of ways, such as dotting or dabbing the nib against the wooden surface, or moving it around in a random, haphazard arrangement of lines and scribbles.

6

Add definition to the texture. Add depth and definition to the texture by adding dots and lines to the bangle with a spoon point nib on a high temperature setting. You can add more areas of shadow or use dots to make the surface appeared more rough and pitted. The unshaded letters and borders should now stand out clearly.

Tools and Materials

- 1 shaped wooden plaque blank
- Several small blank wooden craft shapes to suit your theme
- Hand drill and bit
- Pencil and eraser
- Tracing paper
- Masking tape
- Scissors, craft knife, or scalpel
- Pyrography machine
- Writing nib
- Spoon point nib
- Bladed nib
- Several silk cords in three different colors

DOOR HANGER

Patterns on pages 78–79.

Children love making little areas of space their own, whether it's a bedroom, a playroom, or an impromptu fort. They also appreciate gifts that include their own name or something personal to them as a decoration. Door hangers make ideal presents for children, as they can be made just for them and also allow them to have some control over their space. Door hangers can also be used for special occasions, such as Halloween or Christmas, allowing you to let Santa Claus know where you are or to inform children that it's okay to trick or treat at your home!

Wooden hanger blanks are relatively inexpensive and available in a range of shapes and sizes. They are often made of lightweight birch plywood, but you may also be able to purchase customized blanks in solid wood. If you don't want to use a shaped wooden blank with a precut hole (made to fit over a doorknob),

you can buy any wooden blank and make your own hanging mechanism. A drilled hole with ribbon is a good alternative. The benefit of such items is that they can be decorated in an exciting and fun style, making them appealing to young minds or those who are young at heart! Who's to say someone special in your life wouldn't like a sign to hang on his or her study, workroom, or bedroom door?

My door hanger uses a Halloween theme, combined with a little imagination, to create a unique door sign. You could easily apply the same techniques to make a sign for any theme or occasion. For example, add paint in various shades of pink or blue for a child's bedroom sign, or add some festive colors for a Christmas hanger. Give this project a go and then design your own version!

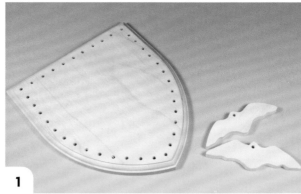

1 Drill holes in the wooden pieces. Drill ¹⁄₁₆"–¹⁄₈" (2–3mm)-diameter holes at regular intervals around the edge of the plaque, leaving a gap of about ⅜" (10mm) between each hole. Drill a ¹⁄₁₆"–¹⁄₈" (2–3mm)-diameter hole at the top of each small craft shape so they can be hung from the main plaque.

2 Transfer the design. Trace your chosen design and lettering onto tracing paper and transfer it to the main plaque, using masking tape to secure it in place. Draw additional detail onto each of the small craft shapes to make them more interesting: do this on both sides if you wish.

3 Burn the lettering. Use a writing nib on a high temperature setting to burn the outside edges of the lettering on the plaque. To give my letters a spooky, Halloween appearance, I stayed away from neat, precise marks and made a series of deep, dark, and irregular marks to add to the feel and appearance of the overall design.

4 Burn the design. Use a bladed nib on a medium/high setting to burn the outline of your plaque design and the detail on the small craft shapes. Try to keep these lines as crisp as you can, taking time to ensure each connecting mark meets up smoothly with the next as you turn the blank to work comfortably.

5 Add texture and shading. Use your spoon point nib to build up shading anywhere on your plaque design and craft shapes. Use high temperature settings and extended surface application to create dark areas, and the opposite to create light areas. Use stippled or broken marks to add texture and variety wherever you feel it is appropriate.

6 Create the hanger. Now, on to the cords! Thread the cords in and out of the holes along the edges of the plaque as you desire, leaving the cord tails hanging down at the bottom of the plaque so the craft shapes can be attached to them. If desired, braid the cords together between the top corners of the plaque to create a loop for hanging the plaque on a hook, or leave the cords unbraided.

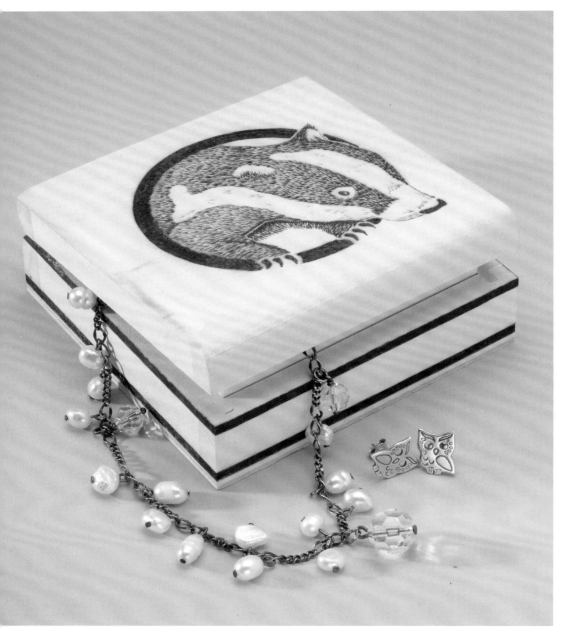

Tools and Materials

- 1 small blank wooden box
- Pencil and eraser
- Ruler
- Compass
- Tracing paper
- Masking tape
- Scissors, craft knife, or scalpel
- Pyrography machine
- Spear nib
- Spoon point nib
- Bladed nib

JEWELRY BOX

Patterns on page 80.

There is something intrinsically pleasing about small boxes that I have always found inexplicably appealing. I'm sure I'm not the only one who has put a tiny box in a drawer for a day in the future when it might prove useful for some unknown purpose! A beautifully decorated miniature box can sometimes be just as appealing as the contents it protects. We often give presents like rings, earrings, and bracelets to our loved ones on special occasions, but these gifts are often packaged in mass-produced anonymous boxes. Why not take the time to design and make a personalized box that will contain as much sentimental value as the gift itself?

Blank wooden boxes are available at all good craft stores in a variety of shapes and sizes. They can be purchased with hinged lids, or lids that lift free from the body of the box. In addition to rectangular boxes made

of flat sections of wood, you can purchase round boxes turned on a lathe. Rounded boxes provide a completely different challenge when considering a pyrography design for them. Keep in mind that the smaller the box, the harder it will be to handle while you burn, so select a larger box if you are just starting out, or make sure you watch out for your fingers!

Animal portraits are a popular subject for most pyrographers, but if you are just beginning, working on a large design can be daunting. The purpose of this project is to introduce you to the techniques used to create fur or feathers at a more manageable scale than a full-sized portrait. See Chapter 3 for some alternative images you can practice burning before you move on to developing your own patterns from photographs or similar items.

1

Make a border and transfer the animal design. Measure and mark the center point of the box lid. Using a compass, draw two circles, one inside the other, on the box lid to create a ring approximately ³⁄₁₆"–⁵⁄₁₆" (5–8mm) thick. Draw two sets of parallel lines around the sides of the box body to make a border. Trace and transfer your animal design into the ring.

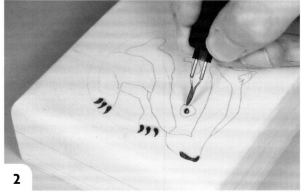

2

Burn the details. Use a spear nib on a high temperature setting to burn in the darkest areas of detail, such as the claws, eye, and nose of the badger. The point of the spear nib allows you to create detailed, precise marks on a small scale.

3

Burn the fur texture. Use the lip of a spoon point nib on a medium/high setting to create the fur texture by making short, consistent lines moving in a realistic direction. Use a small flicking motion repeatedly, with each small line building up a furry texture. Do not press too hard so the lines remain thin and delicate.

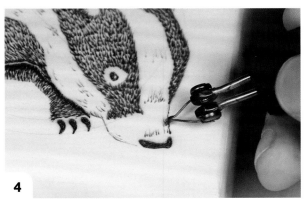

4

Add shading detail. Add dark areas of shading for increased definition, such as under the chin to define the obscured leg. Use a small number of soft lines to add texture to lighter areas like the white band down the nose. Add a row of small lines to create a soft outline where needed, rather than one solid line.

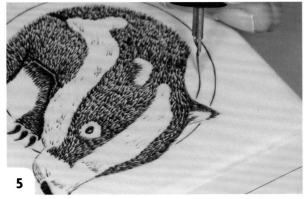

5

Outline the ring and borders. Outline the ring around the badger and the borders on the sides of the box with a bladed nib on a medium/high temperature setting. Keep the lines as neat and crisp as possible, ensuring that they join smoothly wherever you need to stop and restart burning.

6

Fill in the ring and borders. Use the bowl of a spoon point nib to shade the ring and the borders on the side of the box with a dark, even, shaded tone. These shaded areas help frame the design and add interest to the box itself, so try not to burn over the outlines. Once finished, erase any visible pencil marks.

Tools and Materials

- 1 blank/untreated wooden photo frame
- Pencil and eraser
- Ruler
- Tracing paper
- Masking tape
- Scissors, craft knife, or scalpel
- Pyrography machine
- Bladed nib
- Spoon point nib
- Shading nib

PHOTO FRAME

Patterns on pages 81–82.

Photo frames are probably the most popular commissioned item I am requested to make. A personalized frame for a couple on their wedding day, complete with their names, wedding date, and a decorative design, is an ideal gift that will be cherished forever. A photo frame can be designed specifically to display an image for a whole host of special occasions, or simply decorated to create a unique handmade frame without any particular occasion in mind.

Frames come in a variety of shapes and dimensions, including rectangular or round shapes. When purchasing a frame for pyrography, make sure the frame has not been treated or varnished in any way. Treated frames can be difficult to burn or can give off harmful fumes

during burning, so check your local craft stores for blank, untreated wooden frames. If you know of a local frame manufacturer, it never hurts to ask if they will supply you with untreated frames. After all, it gives them less work to do! You may also be able to make a similar arrangement with an online supplier.

This project uses a simple silhouette theme to create a bold and striking border design. The safari-theme picture frame would make a great gift for someone who loves wild animals or has perhaps gone on a safari vacation. The principles of this style can easily be applied to any number of themes or subjects to allow you to create your own customized frames.

1

Create a border. Using a ruler and pencil, draw border lines ⅛" (3mm) from the inner and outer edges of the photo frame. The border marks the area in which you will burn your design. Do not press too hard when drawing the lines, as they will be erased when the frame is finished.

2

Burn the inner border. Using a bladed nib on a medium/high temperature setting, burn along the lines for the inner border. Make sure the lines are as neat and straight as possible, especially where they meet at the corners. Work your way around all four inside edges.

3

Add shading. Use a spoon point nib on a medium/ high temperature setting to create a protective border of shading along the line of the inner border. Work from the inner border line out toward the outer edge of the frame with the bowl of the nib to build up a dark area of tone, taking care not to go over the line.

4

Trace your design. Draw or print your frame images at the correct size for the area in which you will be burning. If necessary, resize the images on your computer or using a photocopier. Trace the outline of each image in pencil onto tracing paper, ready to be transferred. You can draw the designs freehand if you prefer.

5

Transfer the design. Decide how many images you want on each side of your frame. Place and transfer each design, one by one, scribbling on the reverse side of the tracing paper to transfer the design outline. Make sure you place the bottom edge of each image along the line of the inner border. Work your way around each side of the frame until you have transferred the desired number of images.

6

Add a corner design. Use your pencil to draw a freehand design that matches the theme of your frame in each corner. For my safari frame, I added a tree trunk. These corner designs will help the border design flow around the frame more naturally, and keeps you from having to arrange an animal at the frame's corners or leave them blank.

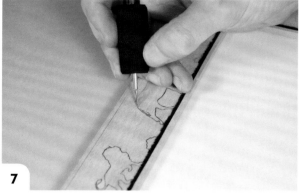

7

Outline the border images. Using a bladed nib on a medium/high temperature setting, burn the outlines of each border image in turn. Adjust the position of the frame or the angle you are working at regularly to ensure you are working in a comfortable position with the pen at a natural angle in relation to your hand.

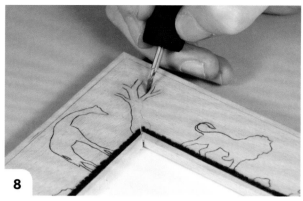

8

Outline the corner images. Using the bladed nib at a medium/high temperature setting, burn the outline of each corner image. Add any desired details between each animal, such as the outline of small rocks, to add more visual interest to the flow of the border.

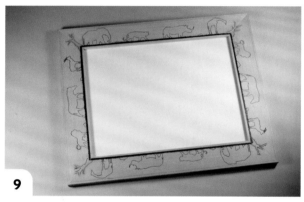

9

Double check the design. Once you have finished the outlines of all the images on every side of the frame, check the whole composition to ensure you are satisfied with the layout before you move on to shading the images. Add any further details until you are happy with the overall appearance.

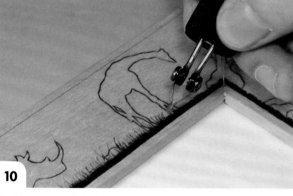

10

Add ground texture. Set your pyrography machine to a high setting and use the lip of the spoon point nib in a series of quick, flicking motions, lifting the nib from the wood as you do so. This creates a texture to represent long grass on the safari frame. Change direction and add kinked lines for a random effect. Use a different texture to fit your frame's theme, such as seaweed or waves for an ocean theme.

11

Begin shading the images. Use the bowl of the spoon point nib to start shading around the inside of each image outline. Work slowly and carefully to build up a protective border of dark shading, moving away from each outline into the center of the image, without crossing over the outline marks.

12

Add detail shading. Use the lip and edge of the spoon point nib to shade in any acute angles, fine lines, or sharply detailed areas, such as the horns of the rhino or the narrow legs of the giraffe. The goal is to shade the inside of each image to create a silhouette, while maintaining the crisp outline.

13

Add detail to the corner designs. Use the spoon point nib on a high temperature setting to add detail to your corner designs. I created foliage for my trees in each corner by using a random dotting motion repeatedly. This creates a textured surface to give the impression of leaves. Add detail shading to your corner designs until you are happy with their appearance.

14

Create the silhouettes. Use a broad shading nib to fill in the unshaded areas of any image to be filled with solid tone. Note: Don't fill in any areas where you want to add a pattern or texture, such as the body of the tiger, where you might want to add stripes.

15

Add patterns or texture. Use the spoon point nib on a medium/high temperature setting to add a pattern or texture to any unshaded images. You can add patterns to resemble markings for zebras, tigers, giraffes, and more, as this will add interest and intricacy to your finished design.

16

Burn the outer border. Use the flat face of a bladed nib at a high temperature setting to create a patterned edge around the outside of the frame. Place the tip against the wood at regular intervals, moving along each edge, using the pencil line for the outer border as a guide to keep the design neat. Work around the frame, and then erase the pencil lines.

Further suggestions

Photo frames provide you with a great opportunity to express yourself creatively. This project is aimed at making the crafter think about the layout and considerations for working on a frame as a canvas. The frame's shape itself brings its own benefits and drawbacks due to the narrow working area. As already mentioned, you can design your own commemorative frames for special occasions or events, utilizing text, images, patterns, and more to make your own decorative style.

You can develop this project by moving from silhouette designs to more realistic imagery, with textural shading, as your confidence and abilities improve. Consider what the frame is to be used for and try to develop a design that will work with the displayed content so that each enhances the other. Intricate border designs, such as Celtic knotwork or floral garlands, can also make extremely beautiful and desirable subjects for picture frames. Experiment with the composition of repeated motifs to inspire your own pyrography style. Alternative themes, such as graffiti or Steampunk, may also provide you with ideas for your own designs.

Tools and Materials

- 1 blank circular wooden plate or plaque

- Pencil and eraser

- Tracing paper

- Masking tape

- Compass

- Scissors, craft knife, or scalpel

- Pyrography machine

- Bladed nib

- Spoon point nib

- Spear nib

- Shading nib

DECORATIVE PLATE

Patterns on pages 83–85.

Decorative plates or plaques are almost as popular as personalized photo frames in terms of the number of commissions I receive for them. As a pyrographer, I love working on these items, as they form a perfect smooth canvas, just calling out to be decorated in some way. Plates can be decorated in any theme you wish, incorporating any combination of text, images, patterns, or texture. When completed, such items can be displayed on a table or in a cabinet, or they can be mounted on a wall.

Suppliers for blank plaques and plates are easily found, and such items are generally competitively priced, which makes them a good project choice for a new crafter. The most inexpensive plaques may be made from birch plywood or a similar material, in a range of shapes and sizes with plain edging, while more

expensive plates can be found in a solid wood with shaped edges or a rim. The lip or rim of a plate can be useful as a ready-made frame to enclose the edge of a pyrography design, eliminating the need to draw your own border. You may be able to have plates turned to your specifications if you know of a woodturner in your area.

The plate featured in this project uses a Celtic heart motif with a natural leaf border, displayed against a dark background for visual impact. The finishing touch is an old Scottish saying in a font that matches the general style of the whole piece. There are a number of alternative visual elements available in Chapter 3 so you can tailor the project to suit your own preferences or that of the recipient.

1

Draw or transfer the central design. Draw your central design on the center area of the plate, or use tracing paper to transfer it directly onto the wood. If you plan to trace and transfer it, be certain that you have adjusted the size of the image using your computer or a photocopier so the scale of the design fits the plate.

2

Outline the central design. Use a bladed nib at a medium/high temperature setting to burn the outline of your central design. For the Celtic knot, the success of the design is wholly reliant on smooth lines and neat intersections, so take your time and burn the lines evenly and without rushing them.

3

Draw or transfer your decorative design. Draw or trace and transfer your decorative design around your central design. I used an ivy garland design. When transferring your decorative designs onto the wood, do not transfer any areas of the design located behind the central design because you will not need to burn these.

4

Outline the decorative design. Use the bladed nib at a medium/high setting to draw the outline of the decorative design. Take your time, as ornate decorative designs can contain areas with closely paired parallel lines and acute angles. Work your way around the design, ensuring your lines don't cross over the outline of the central design.

5

Shade the plate border. Use the bowl of a spoon point nib on a medium/high setting to create a protective border of shading around the inner rim of the turned plate. If your plate has a flat surface with no shaped edging, you can create this edge visually by drawing a border and shading along the inner edge of the line.

6

Begin shading the background. Use a spear nib on a medium/high setting to start filling in your dark background behind the central and decorative designs. The spear nib will allow you to shade inside any acute angles or sharp areas where a broader nib might inadvertently cross your existing outline design.

7

Continue shading the background. Continue to add shading using the bowl of a spoon point nib around the remaining unshaded outlines. Once complete, all lines located next to an area of dark background should have some protective shading along one edge.

8

Finish shading the background. You are now ready to fill in the remaining areas of dark background using a broad shading nib on a medium/high temperature setting. Work your way around the designs, shading in each required area until the background is completely filled and only the central and decorative designs remain unshaded.

9

Draw in the detail. Use a pencil to lightly draw in some detail on your decorative design. I chose to add veins to each individual leaf of the ivy garland. Draw a central vein down the center of each leaf, and surround it with parallel lines radiating from the middle. Refer to photographs of actual leaves for a realistic look if this helps you build up the design.

10

Shade the decorative design. Use the bowl of a spoon point nib on a low/medium setting to add shading to your decorative design. I shaded each leaf of the ivy garland in turn. Start with the nib next to the central vein and lightly drag it toward the edge of the leaf between each radiating line, adding soft shading while leaving the lines free of any burning for contrast.

11

Shade the central design. Use a bladed nib on a low/medium setting to add definition and depth to the central design. Add shading by lightly dragging the nib in parallel lines to create shadow where parts of the design cross over other sections, creating a three-dimensional look.

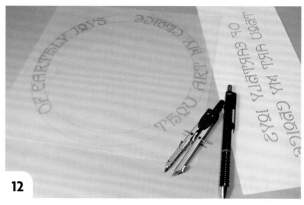

12

Trace the lettering. Prepare the layout for the plate rim lettering by creating a ring of concentric circles the size of your plate rim on tracing paper. Then trace each letter of your desired quote into the ring individually. This allows you to cut each section of the quote from the tracing paper individually and lay the quote out on the plate symmetrically.

13

Align the text. Cut your quote out in sections and secure the tracing paper to the desired place on the plate with masking tape. Adjust the position until the design looks correct to your eye. Drawing a centerline on the plate to be matched up with a centerline drawn through the middle of the lettering can help you achieve the proper alignment.

14

Transfer the text. Scribble on the back side of the tracing paper to transfer the lettering onto the wooden plate. Work carefully so that you don't dislodge the tracing paper or produce a smudged transfer of the letters. Remove the masking tape and tracing paper carefully once you have finished.

15

Shade the letters. Fill in each letter with a soft stippled texture using the point of a spear nib on a medium/high setting. This adds an aged, antique look to the lettering, which fits in with the general feel of the Celtic knot design. Work carefully and precisely within the pencil outline of the letters. If you chose a different design, shade your letters to match its style.

16

Add a border. Use the tip of the spear point nib on a high temperature setting to create a scalloped pattern around the plate's edge. Work steadily, applying the nib to the surface of the wood at regular intervals for a few seconds. If desired, draw a pencil guideline to work up to (like you did for the picture frame border on page 43) if this makes you feel more confident in achieving an even finish.

Further suggestions

The possibilities for building on the principles demonstrated in this project in order to generate your own unique designs are literally infinite. The lip or rim of the plate can contain a range of text or commemorative messages, so you can present a plaque to someone to remind them of a certain occasion or achievement. Mixing and matching from a selection of visual elements allows you to experiment with composition and create designs that are varied on a theme. Try collecting a visual library of favorite images so you have something to refer to when working on a new design.

As your skills in pyrography increase, you may want to move on to drawing your own images, such as landscapes or portraits, in the central area of a plate. Portraits of animals are always popular, or you may wish to work from photographs to draw members of your family. My first book, *Woodburning with Style*, contains a number of chapters and projects that can help you expand your abilities in this area if it is of interest to you.

Tools and Materials

- 1 blank wooden box
- Pencil and eraser
- Ruler
- Compass
- Tracing paper
- Masking tape
- Scissors, craft knife, or scalpel
- Hand drill and bit
- Pyrography machine
- Bladed nib
- Spoon point nib
- Writing nib
- Acrylic paints of your choice
- Paintbrushes
- Water
- Palette or mixing plate
- 1 decorative metal handle with fixings

KEEPSAKE BOX

Patterns on pages 86–87.

It is far too easy to get caught up in the buzz of day-to-day life and overlook the things of emotional importance. A small item, such as a birthday card, a note from a loved one, or a drawing by a child, can easily get swept up amidst the everyday bills, receipts, invoices, and paperwork. These sentimental items are easy to misplace, but impossible to replace. I recently completed a commission for a gentleman who asked me to design a large memory box as a gift to his wife so she could safely store all the poems he had written for her during their forty years of marriage. It was a pleasure to create something so meaningful that will probably be passed on through their family as part of their personal history.

As previously mentioned, blank boxes are readily available from craft stores in a range of shapes and sizes. Consider what items you intend to store in your box and select one in a size to suit that need. You might also consider whether you want a lid that lifts off completely or is hinged, and whether you want a box with a clasp or locking mechanism. Some boxes available have a fabric lining or drawer compartments to help protect smaller treasured possessions.

This project will teach you about the best way to develop designs using complicated patterns, such as Celtic knotwork, around a three-dimensional object. It also uses color and metal embellishments to add a little variety to the finished design.

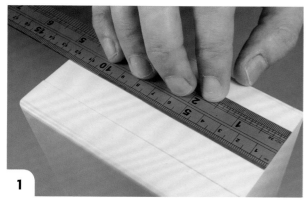

1

Measure the box. To add a Celtic border to your box, measure the circumference of your box with a ruler or tape measure and divide the total measurement into equal segments. Square boxes are easy because they have four equal sides, but a rectangular box may need to be divided into four or six sections of equal size to allow you to create your Celtic border accurately.

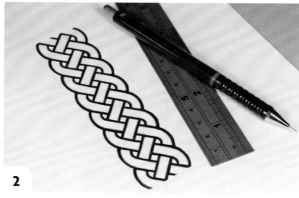

2

Size and trace the border segment. Using your computer or a photocopier, print out the knotwork border at the required size. The patterns provided in this book have been drawn to fit together seamlessly when placed next to one another repeatedly. Trace the border onto tracing paper.

3

Transfer the first segment. Secure the tracing paper with the knotwork border to one side of the box with masking tape, ready to be transferred. Fold the tracing paper around the corner of the box if a section of the design needs to wrap around the corner to be completed. Scribble on the reverse side of the tracing paper to transfer the drawing onto the wood.

4

Finish transferring the border. Repeat the process described in Step 3 to transfer the traced knotwork segment again, making sure the edge lines up with the first transfer. Repeat transferring the border around the box until you have successfully created a full border of knotwork that runs continuously around every side of the box.

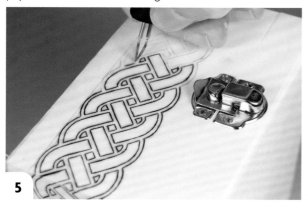

5

Burn the outline. Use a bladed nib on a medium/high temperature setting to burn the outline of the Celtic knotwork border. Keep the lines as crisp as you can, and ensure that all the lines remain parallel wherever possible so they appear even and consistent in thickness once shaded.

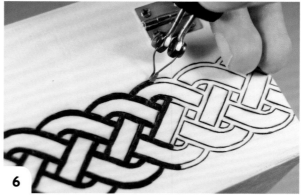

6

Fill in the outline. Change to a spoon point nib on a medium/high setting and start to shade within the outline of the knotwork border, carefully filling the lines with a solid, even tone. Take care not to shade over any lines made with the bladed nib, because this can ruin the appearance of the design.

Learn to Burn

7

Shade the knotwork. Turn the temperature down to a low/medium setting. Use the spoon point nib to create shading in the body of the knotwork, producing a tone that fades from dark (where a line crosses under another line) to light (at the high points where a line crosses over another line). Drag and lift the nib for a gradual tone.

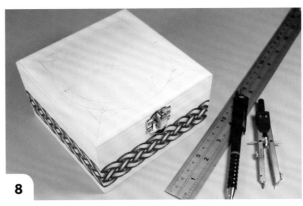

8

Create a border. Construct a simple border on the top and sides of the box lid using a ruler and a compass. You can also place a thin border along the top edge of the box body. For the lid, create a rectangular frame with a ring on top. The border lines should be as thick as the metal handle you've chosen for the box, and the ring's diameter should equal the handle's width.

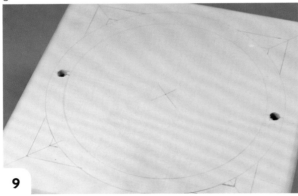

9

Drill the handle holes. Mark and drill two holes in the box lid so the metal handle can be fixed securely to it. Make sure you measure carefully to drill holes of the correct diameter and the correct width apart. Creating the lid border based on the dimensions of the metal handle will help visually incorporate the handle into the design.

10

Shade the borders. Use a writing nib on a medium/high temperature setting to fill the lid borders with a dotted, stippled shading effect. Keep the spread and density of the dots as even and consistent as possible for an even tone. Erase any pencil lines that are still visible once the shading is complete.

11

Transfer the lid insect design. Trace your chosen lid insect design and transfer it into place on the lid of the box. Select a small design, as the goal of the decoration is to create a delicate area of interest that might lead someone to take a second look when they see the box, causing them to question if the insect is real or drawn!

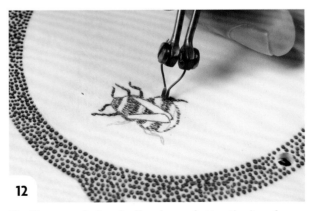

12

Outline and shade the insect. Use the lip of a spoon point nib on a medium setting to draw the main features and details of the insect. Try to use a combination of small, broken lines to give the insect as much visual texture as possible.

13

Paint the insect body. Select an appropriate color of acrylic paint for the body of the insect you have chosen. Mix the paint on your palette with a small amount of water to thin it slightly before painting the body of your insect. Thinning the paint a little will ensure the pyrography marks show through the color.

14

Paint the wings. Use thinned white acrylic paint to add some highlights to the wings of your insect design. Once the white paint has dried, you can always draw some lines over the wings with pencil to add some detailed, realistic texture to their appearance.

15

Paint the shadow. Add a tiny amount of brown acrylic paint to a few drops of water to create a very thin brown wash. Apply this around the edges of your insect to create a shadow. This will help give the design a three-dimensional look, as if the insect has just stopped briefly on the lid of the box.

16

Attach the handle. Once the paint has dried, attach your decorative handle to the lid using the screws provided and the holes you drilled during Step 9. Your keepsake box is now complete and ready for use.

Further suggestions

This project uses only a tiny amount of color in combination with the pyrography marks, but even this small touch of detail demonstrates the potential for you to explore with this technique. As you develop your own larger and more ambitious pyrography projects, you may wish to explore the use of materials like acrylic paints and colored inks in combination with your burnt lines and marks. Customizing your wooden box blanks with ready-made metal accessories can also create a specific feel or appearance. Keep your eyes peeled for these items when browsing in craft stores or online.

Three-dimensional objects present their own particular challenges in terms of composition and layout. Creating a design that flows successfully around a form, rather than a flat surface, is a skill in itself. Through careful planning, you can create designs that enhance every plane of an item, inviting people to admire the object from several angles. Tracing the various elements onto different pieces of tracing paper allows you to adjust the positioning and scale. This also keeps you from wasting time by drawing and erasing your designs directly on your project until you are satisfied with them.

Tools and Materials

- 1 blank clock kit (including a wooden face, clock mechanism, and hands)

- Pencil and eraser

- Ruler

- Compass

- Protractor/angle measurer

- Tracing paper

- Masking tape

- Scissors, craft knife, or scalpel

- Pyrography machine

- Bladed nib

- Spear nib

- Spoon point nib

- Green ink

- Paintbrush

- Hand drill and bit

- 12 antique brass upholstery pins

WALL CLOCK

Patterns on pages 88–90.

A beautifully designed clock can be a welcome addition to any room. Making your own clock allows you the freedom to create something to suit the style and feel of the surroundings in which it will be displayed. The decorative style of the clock is only limited by your creative imagination. With just a little consideration, your handmade clock can be elegant, bold, subtle, dramatic, beautiful, striking, ominous, light-hearted, or thought-provoking, as well as capable of telling the time! You can design a clock for a child's bedroom, a kitchen, an office, or any other area. The location of your clock will help determine the requirements for it in terms of design, composition, and appearance.

Many craft suppliers sell clock kits, which contain a shaped wooden clock face, along with all of the required hands and mechanical components to form

the clock movement. Wooden clock faces themselves are generally available in a range of sizes and shapes, many with decorative routed edging to give the clock a more finished appearance. It is best to decorate the face of your clock and treat it with your desired finish before you assemble the movement.

For this project, you will create a decorative clock using some of my favorite tribal tattoo styles, a recurring theme in my *Wood Tattoos* pyrography portfolio! Chapter 3 contains some alternative design styles for you to use if you wish to try a slightly different appearance. For a successful design, consider the style of the clock hands and metal pins you select so that they complement each other in the finished piece.

1

Mark the clock face. Using your protractor and ruler, measure out and mark the clock face, dividing it into twelve equal sections to show the numerical points. The angle of each section should be 30°. Lightly draw the section lines in pencil. This will help you keep the required structure of the clock face design.

2

Begin transferring the border design. Draw or print your chosen border design for the clock at the correct size for your clock face blank. Trace the design onto tracing paper and transfer it into position on the clock face by scribbling on the reverse side. Note: The clock patterns for this book have been divided into quarters.

3

Finish transferring the border design. Repeat the process of tracing and transferring your border design onto each subsequent quarter of the clock face, making sure the sections match up precisely. The original tracing may become faint if used too often, so you may need to retrace from your original printout onto a new piece of tracing paper occasionally.

4

Outline the border design. Use a bladed nib on a medium/high temperature setting to draw the outline of the border design, working your way around the whole clock to complete the design as one full, connected border. Keep your lines even, sharp, and consistent, making sure you don't catch or snag the nib in the wood.

5

Create the central design. Once the border is completed, select your central design. Size the design to match your clock face and trace it for transferring onto the clock. Make sure your design allows for the hole in the center of the clock, as well as the space that will be taken up by the clock movement, so the design's detail is not lost or obscured by any of the clock parts.

6

Transfer the central design. Place the tracing paper in position and scribble on the reverse side to transfer the design outline onto the wooden surface of the clock. Take care not to move the tracing paper during this process, as this may distort the image and force you to start again. Use masking tape to hold the paper in place.

7

Burn the central design outline. Use the bladed nib on a medium/high temperature setting to draw the outline of the central design. Do your best to ensure the lines remain neat and fluid, even when you need to stop and restart burning in the middle of a long line. Erase any remaining pencil lines.

8

Shade the design points. Use a spear nib on a medium/high setting to start the shading process in any areas where the lines are very close together or form a point. Shading these areas with a broad nib might lead to mistakes and inaccuracies. Work your way around the whole design until all such areas are shaded.

9

Shade the design outline. Use a spoon point nib on a medium/high setting to continue the shading, creating a shaded border along the bladed nib outlines of the border and central design. The bowl of the nib should be used to shade away from the outlines as carefully as possible, working into the areas to be shaded.

10

Finish shading the border design. Keeping the spoon point nib at the same temperature setting, fill in the border design by creating a dense, stippled, textural pattern. Press the bowl of the nib repeatedly into the wood's surface, keeping the marks as close together as possible without creating a solid tone.

11

Shade the central design. Continue adding darker shading to the central dragon image to give the impression of form and solidity. Use the bowl of the spoon point nib on a medium/high setting to increase the dark tone wherever you feel it appropriate to create shadow and depth.

12

Draw in additional detail. Use a pencil to lightly draw in additional detail in the remaining unshaded areas of the central design. For the dragon, draw a simple scale pattern in rows around the rest of the body, while adding lines for hair or something similar around the head and crest.

13

Burn the added detail. Use a spear nib at a high temperature setting to burn the detail on your central design, working over the pencil lines you drew previously. For the dragon, the lines do not have to be neat or crisp. Dark, scorched lines will add definition in a more appropriate way for the dragon design, particularly in view of the color that is to be applied.

14

Paint the design. Use a paintbrush to carefully apply your chosen ink color to your design. In the case of the dragon, the areas of burnt shading will help to contain the color and prevent bleeding, while the dark lines of the scales and other details will show through the ink clearly. Two coats may be needed for a bold, bright finish.

15

Drill holes for the hour markers. Use a small drill bit (approximately 1/32" [1mm] in diameter) to drill twelve holes in the clock face to mark the position of each number. Place the clock face on a scrap piece of wood during drilling to avoid ruining your table or worktop. For stability, ask someone to hold it for you while you drill.

16

Insert the pins. Gently push an upholstery pin as far as you can into each drilled hole. You may need to use a small hammer or mallet to put them in fully: make sure you only tap the pins lightly to avoid damaging them or splitting the clock face. You are now ready to finish the clock by assembling the mechanism on the rear and fitting the clock hands.

Further suggestions

The scope for what you can do to design your own decorative clocks is vast. You could consider making your own shaped wooden clock faces if you have access to the necessary woodworking equipment, or perhaps you could commission a woodworking associate to make the blanks to your specifications. You could also experiment with drilling into or cutting away sections from blanks that you buy from suppliers to give them a customized individual appearance.

You may also want to look into other materials or items that are available from your local craft or DIY store to see if there is any scope to use them in a decorative way. You might be able to find fixtures or accessories you can use in a visually exciting way, to add depth, color, or texture to your pyrography design in a similar way to the items used in the project above.

Once you start working on your own unique clock designs, it may also be worthwhile to research other suppliers of clock movements. You can purchase clock hands of different shapes, colors, and styles to suit your needs and requirements.

- 1 blank wooden memory album kit

- Several paper/card scrapbook pages

- Pencil and eraser

- Ruler

- Tracing paper

- Masking tape

- Scissors, craft knife, or scalpel

- Several wooden shaped blanks (cogs and letters)

- Fine-grit sandpaper

- Soft cloth

- Wood glue

- Hand drill and bit

- Pyrography machine

- Bladed nib

- Spoon point nib

- Shading nib

- Writing nib

- 1 bracelet chain with a selection of jewelry charms

MEMORY ALBUM

Patterns on page 91.

It is very easy to be overrun by digital technology today. Photographs or mementoes of special occasions can often end up on a hard drive, disc, or other storage device without ever being printed and displayed in an album. A folder of digital images on a screen cannot compete with the physical pleasure of looking through a treasure trove of cherished memories. An album or scrapbook can also be passed on from generation to generation, so why not take the time to create something fitting in which you can display your past?

Memory album kits consist of wooden cover boards that are held together by metal hinges and mounting posts. The front cover is split into two pieces, allowing the cover to be opened with hinges. The mounting posts allow the pages to be held securely, and can be extended to increase the size of the spine so the album

grows as you add more pages. Memory album kits are not as readily available as other kits, so you may need to conduct research to find a supplier. Alternatively, you may be able to make them yourself if you have access to a well-stocked workshop, or find a woodworker who can make them on your behalf.

This project will help you to create a memory album with an alternative steampunk theme. This exciting, fantastical style incorporates a wild visual combination of Victorian and science fiction characteristics with the attitude of the punk movement.

1

Drill the album covers. Place both album covers securely together (you can hold them together with masking tape if desired), and drill a hole at least 5/16" (8mm) in diameter through both in the same place on the side opposite the hinge. Remember to place the covers on a scrap piece of wood to keep from drilling through into your work surface.

2

Sand the covers. Use fine-grit sandpaper to sand every edge and surface of the covers smooth, giving you a suitable surface to burn. Plywood can often have splintered edges, so be careful not to snag your fingers. Use a soft cloth to remove excess dust when you have finished.

3

Draw a border and hinge design. Use a ruler and pencil to draw border lines approximately 3/16"–5/16" (5–8mm) from each edge of the cover and spine. Add detail around the hinges by drawing a shape like a fleur-de-lis, which helps give the impression of an antique book cover. Alternatively, you can trace and transfer a design you like if you don't feel comfortable drawing freehand.

4

Burn the border and hinge design. Use a bladed nib on a medium temperature setting to burn the outline of the hinge design. Birch plywood is fairly soft and can burn very easily, so take your time to ensure the lines are as crisp and sharp as possible. Erase any pencil lines that are still visible once you've finished burning.

5

Draw or transfer your cover design foreground. Draw or transfer your cover design foreground to the front cover of the album. For the steampunk design, trace and transfer the smaller cogs from the pattern for the foreground. Do not press too hard when you scribble on the reverse of the tracing paper during the transferring process, as you may leave an indentation in the soft plywood.

6

Burn the cover design foreground. Use a bladed nib on a medium setting to burn the outline of the front cover design foreground. For the steampunk cover, burn each cog in turn. Shapes like the cogs have a lot of intersections where lines meet at an angle. Try to ensure your lines meet as neatly and precisely as you can manage to make your shapes more successful visually.

7

Draw or transfer the background. Once the foreground design is completed, trace or draw the background design. For the steampunk cover, transfer the large cogs from the pattern. Do not transfer lines of the background design that will be covered by the foreground design in the finished piece.

8

Burn the background design. Use the bladed nib on the same medium setting to burn the outline of the background design. For the steampunk cogs, take care to make sure each cog sits behind the ones in the foreground. Keep your lines sharp and clean, working across the cover to gradually build up the whole design.

9

Shade the design outline. Work around the outline of your cover design, creating a protective shaded border by using a spoon point nib on a medium/high setting. Be careful when working into the angles and forms between each design element and make sure that you do not shade over any of the lines you've already burned.

10

Finish shading the background. Use a broad shading nib to fill in the remaining background areas with a dark, even tone of shading. This helps to lift your design elements and give the whole design a striking effect. This can be time-consuming, as memory album cover blanks can be very large, but stick with it! The effect is worthwhile!

11

Add texture to the foreground design. Use a writing nib on a low temperature setting to create a soft textured effect over the foreground design. For the steampunk cogs, scribble over the surface of each foreground cog to create a random, rough pattern of light lines, building up a tone to fill in the cogs gradually.

12

Shade the background design. Use a spoon point nib on a medium temperature setting to shade the background design in a similar way to the foreground design. For the steampunk cover, work across the surface with scribbled random lines and dots to create a tone that is darker than the foreground cogs, but not as dark as the black background. This variation in tone will create depth in the design.

13

Arrange the wood blanks.

Gather your shaped wooden letters and blanks together and start to arrange them on the front cover. Use the letters to personalize your cover, while using the other shapes to add yet another layer of depth to the design. You could use shapes cut from heavy cardstock if you cannot find suitable wooden blanks.

15

Assemble the album.

Assemble the memory album by fitting the holding posts through the back cover and filling the album with a suitable number of pages. Screw both parts of the front cover together with the hinges. Insert the extension posts if necessary, and then place the front cover on the posts, screwing them in securely.

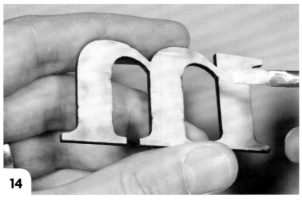

14

Attach the wood blanks.

Apply wood glue to the back of each wooden blank and letter in turn, and put them in place on the album cover. Press down firmly on each blank for a few seconds before moving on to the next one to ensure a good bond. Leave the album somewhere safe and secure while the glue dries.

16

Attach a fastener.

Attach a fastener to your album using the holes you drilled during Step 1. For the steampunk album, make the fastener out of an antique brass bracelet. Use matching jump rings to secure a selection of suitable metal charms to the end of the bracelet containing the clasp.

Further suggestions

I absolutely adored making this project. The pyrography itself is very simple, relying on crisp outlines and textural shading, but the layering of different elements creates a design with a realistic warmth and depth that is fascinating to look at.

You could decorate your own memory album in absolutely any style to make it your own unique design, tailored toward a certain occasion, or made with a cherished person in mind. You could make albums to store memories of weddings, births, academic achievements, holidays, childhood, or any number of other important occasions. Why not make one to act as a portfolio for your woodburning creations?

On the steampunk album, only the front cover was decorated. The back cover is still a blank canvas ready for your own ideas! Why not use the back cover as a place to commemorate the events featured inside the album in the same way the back cover of a book tells you about the contents? You could create an inscription describing the people, location, dates, and other details of the special occasion.

If you are not able to find wooden blanks to suit your design, you could always cut your own with a scroll saw or make them from heavy card stock. Your album could be decorated with colorful inks or metallic paints, as well as any number of craft embellishments to suit your creative vision.

Chapter 3:

Patterns and Gallery

This chapter contains a selection of illustrative designs specific to the fourteen projects in Chapter 2. Each pattern fits in with the theme of the project, and you can pick and choose which you use. You can choose to recreate the projects exactly as described in the step-by-step instructions using the same pattern, or select one of the alternative options to create a slightly different design.

The patterns can either be copied by freehand drawing, traced directly from the book for an exact replica, or photocopied and enlarged if you need to increase the scale to fit the blank you are using. Most of the sample patterns for the larger projects will need to be enlarged, as they have been scaled down to fit the pages of the book. No guidance on scales has been provided, as you will need to determine the size of the patterns you need based on the blank you are planning to use. My first book, *Woodburning with Style,* contains a range of advice on image manipulation methods to assist with your crafting if needed.

A selection of different lettering alphabets are also included for you to use in your designs as needed, as well as a gallery featuring some of my recent *Wood Tattoos* creations to help inspire your own crafting endeavors as you seek to develop a style of your very own after completing the projects in Chapter 2.

GALLERY

This gallery shows you some examples of other designs, projects, and commissions I've completed since the release of *Woodburning with Style*. You can see more of my recent work by visiting my online sites, which are listed in my biography at the beginning of the book.

Alphabet fridge magnets are a great way to keep children entertained while learning. Decorate the blanks with a range of letters to help them spell as they play. You can use any fonts that you like, and you may even decide to experiment with adding color, too.

Larger forms, such as bowls or plates, can be decorated in a sparse or minimal way through carefully placed areas of pattern or texture, forming stylish borders to enhance and complement the natural surface qualities of the wood.

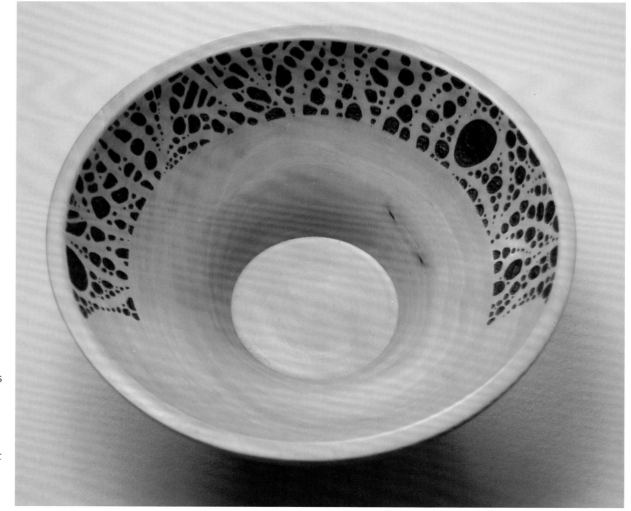

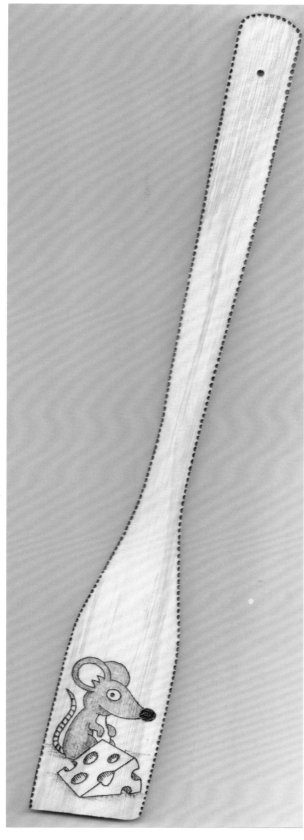

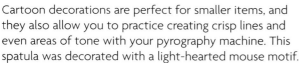

I made this hanging wall plaque using wooden heart blanks that I drilled and fastened with red silk ribbon to make a special gift for Mother's Day from three young children.

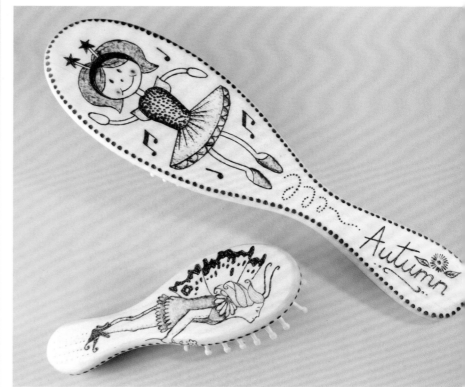

Children love personalized gifts, such as these miniature hairbrushes, decorated with the name of the child and a fairy motif. As your confidence grows, you will be able to make unique presents for all occasions and events.

Cartoon decorations are perfect for smaller items, and they also allow you to practice creating crisp lines and even areas of tone with your pyrography machine. This spatula was decorated with a light-hearted mouse motif.

This wedding frame was created as a unique gift for a couple with the nicknames "Koala" and "Bear." Personalized designs like this ensure that the present will always be treasured.

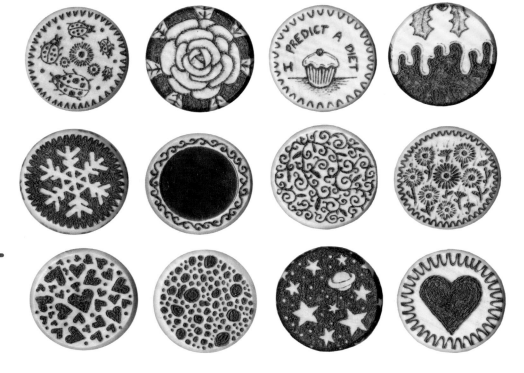

Miniature mirrors are always very popular at the craft fairs where I exhibit my work. They make great gifts at an affordable price. These particular blanks are around 2" (51mm) in diameter, which also helps to improve your pen control due to the amount of detail required.

PATTERNS

The following design patterns can be used on any of the projects included in the book, or for your own pyrography creations.

Napkin Ring Patterns
See page 24 for the Napkin Ring project.

Best Man

Bride

Usher

Bridesmaid

Brother of the

Father of the

Groom

Mother of the

Sister of the

Gift Tag Patterns
See page 26 for the Gift Tag project.

Key Fob Patterns
See page 28 for the Key Fob project.

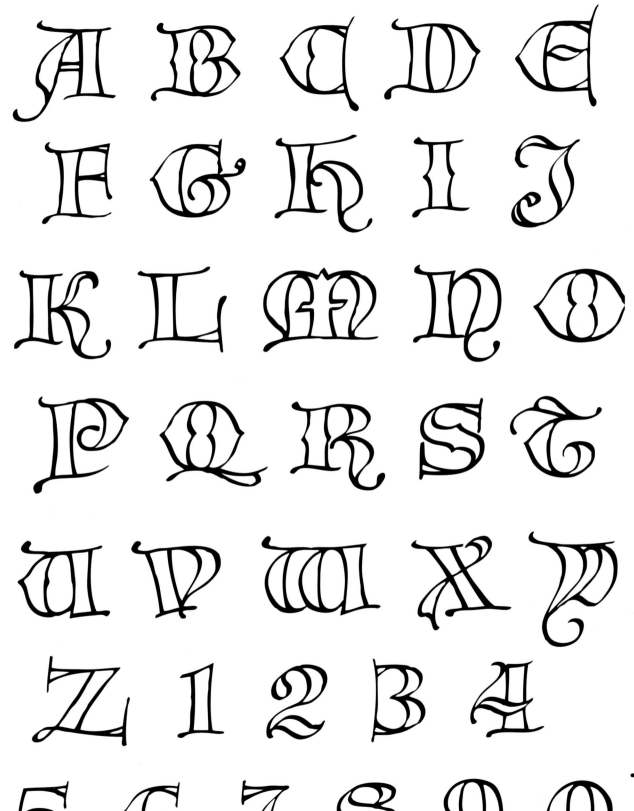

Fridge Magnet Patterns
See page 30 for the Fridge Magnet project.

Table Coaster Patterns
See page 32 for the Table Coaster project.

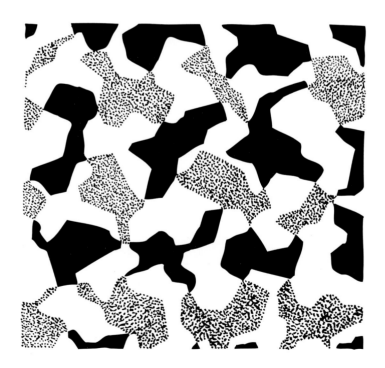

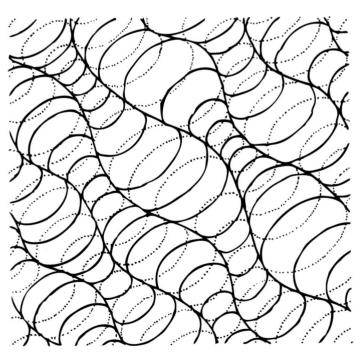

73

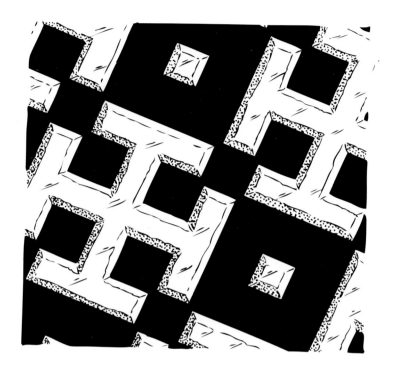

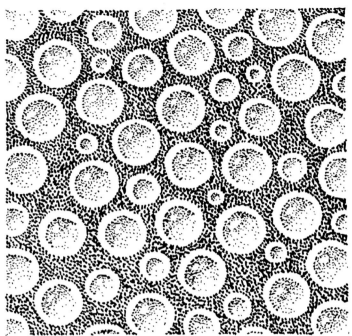

Key Holder Patterns
See page 34 for the Key Holder project.

Bangle Patterns
See page 36 for the Bangle project.
Quote contributions courtesy of Jane Easton.

Our roots entwined, both strong and sure

Grant us laughter, wit... and wine

Let me feel your breath, my love

Sacred journeys begin within

The eyes of beauty belong to you

My wish, my dream, my everything

Face your shadows with courage

TRICK OR TREAT

HAPPY HALLOWEEN!

Pattern courtesy of Chailey Illman.

Pattern courtesy of Chailey Illman.

R.T.P.

Jewelry Box Patterns

See page 40 for the Jewelry Box project.

Photo Frame Patterns
See page 42 for the Photo Frame project.

Decorative Plate Patterns
See page 46 for the Decorative Plate project.

OF EARTHLY JOYS
THOU ART MY CHOICE

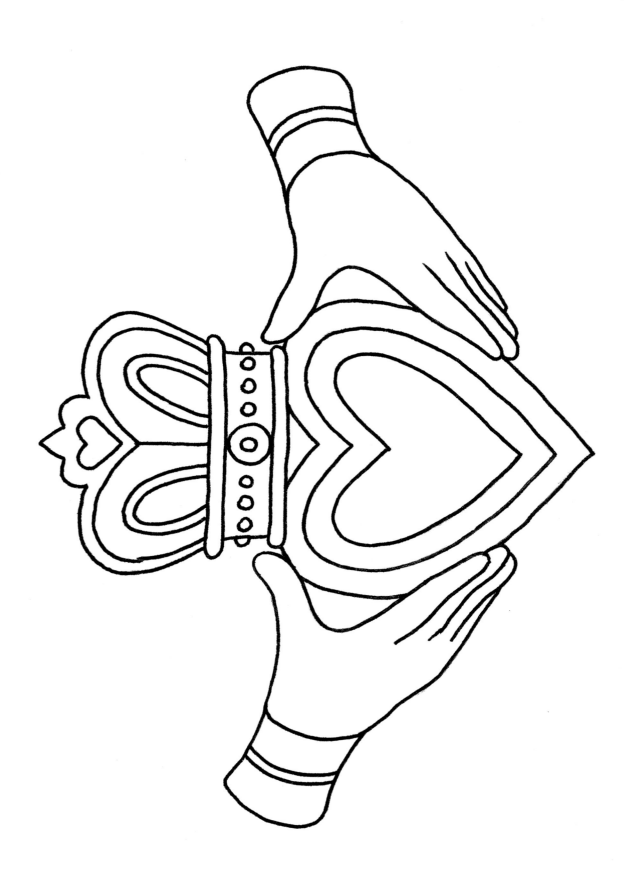

Keepsake Box Patterns

See page 50 for the Keepsake Box project.

Wall Clock Patterns

See page 54 for the Wall Clock project.

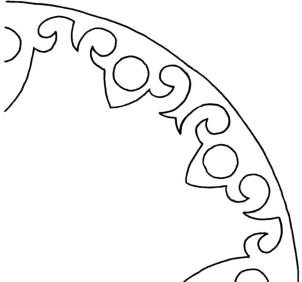

You can alter this dragon pattern by outlining the design instead of shading it.

You can alter this tribal yin-yang pattern
by outlining the design instead of shading it.

Memory Album Pattern
See page 58 for the Memory Album project.

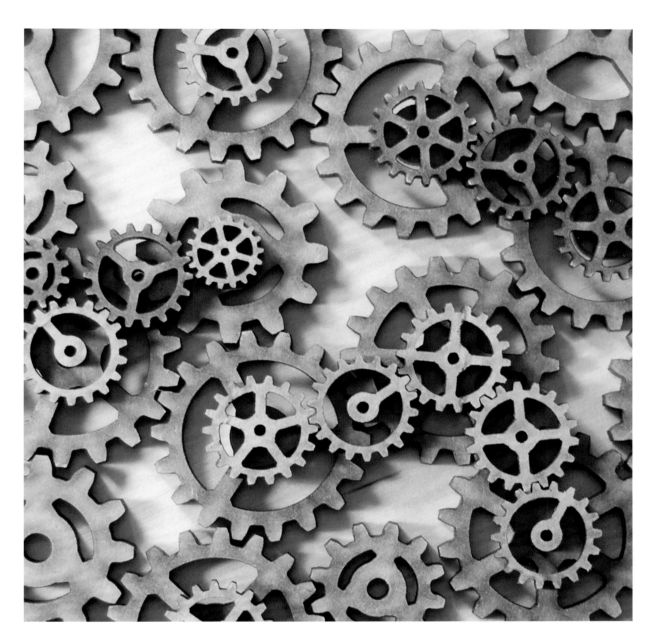

Using this pattern
Start by measuring the size of your memory album cover. Work out how large the pattern needs to be to fill the whole cover. Scan or photocopy the image at the original size and carefully cut it into four equal quarters. You should now be able to scan or photocopy each of the four image sections, resize them on your computer or photocopier, and print them at the enlarged size. You can now piece the enlargement back together like a jigsaw and trace the image, working carefully around each cog outline until you are ready to transfer the design onto your memory album cover for burning.

As well as providing you with an outline, the featured pattern also gives you the opportunity to create three-dimensional shading if you wish by using the tonal values of the photograph so that you can add some realistic depth to your design.

FONTS

The following are several sample fonts you can apply to various projects as you desire. Remember, you can always draw text on a project freehand or use the computer to print a font you like and transfer it onto a project.

ABCDEFGHIJKLMN
OPQRSTUVWXYZ
1234567890
abcdefghijklmn
opqrstuvwxyz.

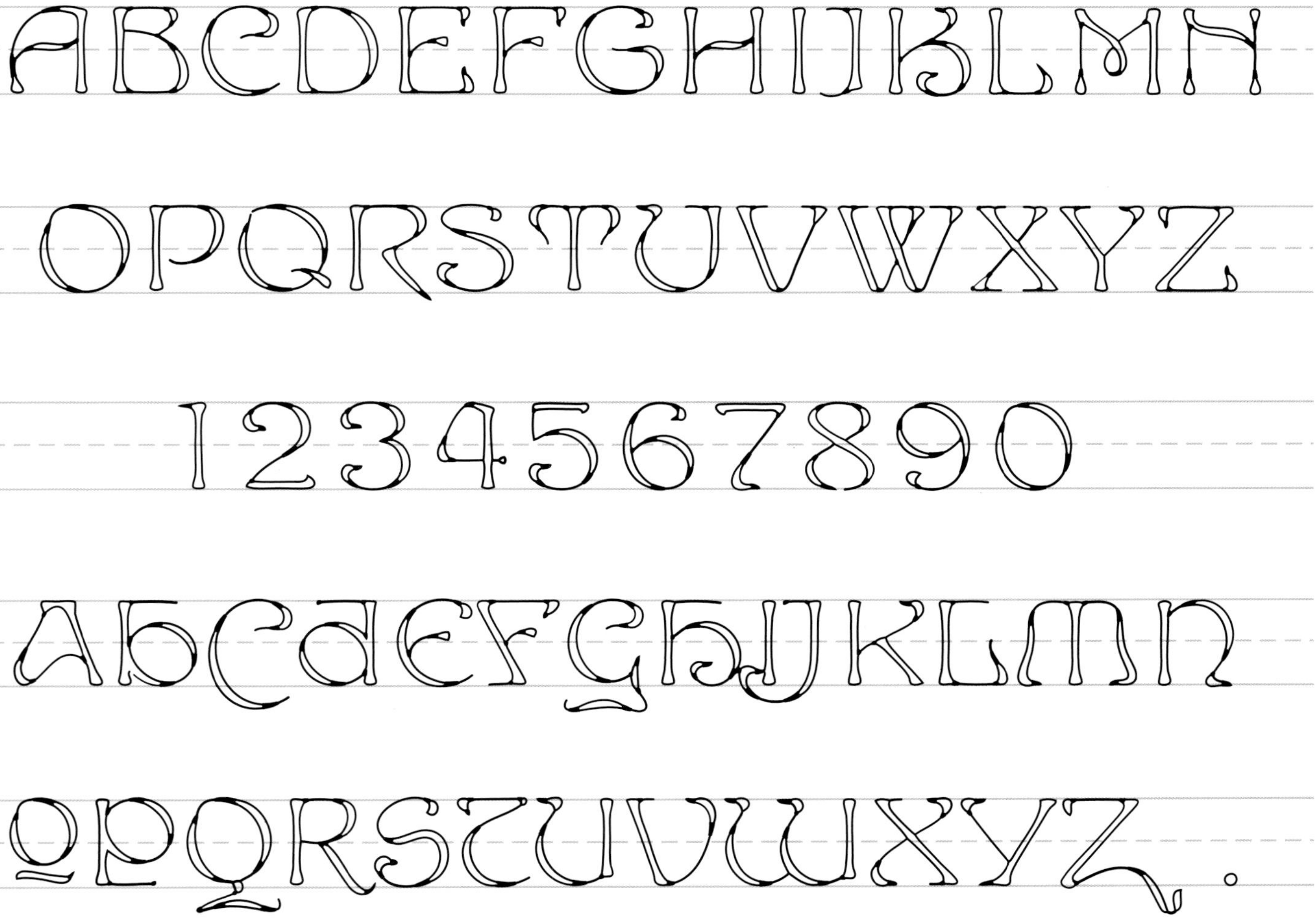

ABCDEFGHIJKLMN

OPQRSTUVWXYZ

1234567890

ABCDEFGHJKLMN

OPQRSTUVWXYZ.

This font was used for the Decorative Plate project (see page 46).

ABCDEF

GHIJKLMN

OPQRSTUVWXYZ

1234567890

abcdefghijklmn

opqrstuvwxyz.

This font was used for the Napkin Rings project (see page 24).

Index

Note: Page numbers in *italics* indicate projects, and page numbers in **bold** indicate patterns.

Acquisition editor: Peg Couch

Copy editors: Paul Hambke and Heather Stauffer

Cover and layout designer: Ashley Millhouse

Cover photographer: Scott Kriner

Editor: Katie Weeber

Proofreader: Lynda Jo Runkle

Indexer: Jay Kreider

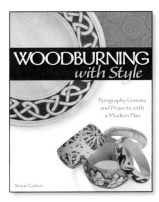

Woodburning with Style
ISBN 978-1-56523-443-7 **$24.95**

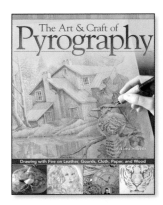

The Art & Craft of Pyrography
ISBN 978-1-56523-478-9 **$19.95**

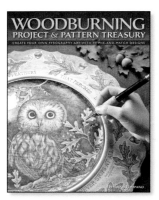

**Woodburning Project
& Pattern Treasury**
ISBN 978-1-56523-482-6 **$24.95**

Great Book of Woodburning
ISBN 978-1-56523-287-7 **$22.95**

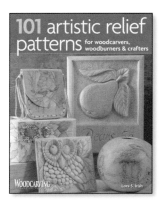

**101 Artistic Relief
Patterns for Woodcarvers,
Woodburners & Crafters**
ISBN 978-1-56523-399-7 **$19.95**

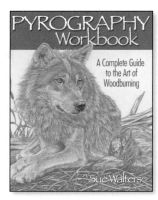

Pyrography Workbook
ISBN 978-1-56523-258-7 **$19.95**

Wood Bangles with Style Kit
ISBN 978-1-56523-610-3 **$19.99**

**Pyrography Workshop
with Sue Walters DVD**
ISBN 978-1-56523-441-3 **$24.95**